DOING POORLY ON PURPOSE

ASCD MEMBER BOOK

Many ASCD members received this book as a member benefit upon its initial release.

Learn more at: **www.ascd.org/memberbooks**

JAMES R. DELISLE

DOING POORLY ON PURPOSE

Strategies to Reverse Underachievement and Respect Student Dignity

ASCD®
Alexandria, VA USA

free spirit
PUBLISHING®

1703 N. Beauregard St.
Alexandria, VA 22311-1714 USA
Phone: 800-933-2723 or 703-578-9600
Fax: 703-575-5400
Website: www.ascd.org
E-mail: member@ascd.org
Author guidelines: www.ascd.org/write

6325 Sandburg Road, Ste. 100
Minneapolis, MN 55427-3674 USA
Website: www.freespirit.com

Deborah S. Delisle, *Executive Director,* Stefani Roth, *Publisher;* Genny Ostertag, *Director, Content Acquisitions;* Julie Houtz, *Director, Book Editing & Production;* Jamie Greene, *Associate Editor;* Masie Chong, *Graphic Designer;* Mike Kalyan, *Director, Production Services;* Kyle Steichen, *Senior Production Specialist;* Keith Demmons, *Senior Production Designer*

Published simultaneously by ASCD and Free Spirit Publishing.

PAPERBACK ISBN: 978-1-4166-2535-3   ASCD product #118023
PDF E-BOOK ISBN: 978-1-4166-2537-7; see Books in Print for other formats.

Quantity discounts: 10–49, 10%; 50+, 15%; 1,000+, special discounts (e-mail programteam@ascd.org or call 800-933-2723, ext. 5773, or 703-575-5773). For desk copies, go to www.ascd.org/deskcopy.

ASCD Member Book No. FY18-1B (Jan. 2015 PS). Member books mail to Premium (P), Select (S), and Institutional Plus (I+) members on this schedule: Jan, PSI+; Feb, P; Apr, PSI+; May, P; Jul, PSI+; Aug, P; Sep, PSI+; Nov, PSI+; Dec, P. For details, see www.ascd.org/membership and www.ascd.org/memberbooks.

Library of Congress Cataloging-in-Publication Data

Names: Delisle, James R., 1953- author.
Title: Doing poorly on purpose : strategies to reverse underachievement and respect student dignity / James Delisle.
Description: Alexandria, Virginia : ASCD, [2018] | Includes bibliographical references and index.
Identifiers: LCCN 2017038836 (print) | LCCN 2017049825 (ebook) | ISBN 9781416625377 (PDF) | ISBN 9781416625353 (pbk).
Subjects: LCSH: Underachievers--Education. | Academic achievement. | Motivation in education.
Classification: LCC LC4661 (ebook) | LCC LC4661 .D45 2018 (print) | DDC 371.2/85--dc23
LC record available at https://lccn.loc.gov/2017038836

26 25 24 23 22 21 20 19 18   1 2 3 4 5 6 7 8 9 10 11 12

DOING POORLY ON PURPOSE

Acknowledgments

Authors never really write books by themselves; instead, they have helpful others behind them who perfect their words and finesse their messages. I was lucky enough to have many such helpful others in completing this book, including:

Jamie Greene, editor extraordinaire, who knew what suggestions to make and questions to ask to make this manuscript as user-friendly as possible.

Darcie Russell, whose guidance with my book's text, illustrations, and cover design was invaluable.

Maureen Marshall, an incredibly passionate artist who made my stories of children and adults come alive through her sensitive, introspective drawings.

and

The students at Scholars Academy in Conway, South Carolina, who provided both the powerful student statements that are sprinkled throughout my book and the perpetual inspiration I need to continue my life as a teacher.

Preface

When I met Matt, he was a 5th grader and I was a first-year teacher. To Matt, school was irrelevant, and he told me so every day by writing that very word—spelled correctly and in red crayon—across the top of any assignment he found personally distasteful. More often than I can recount, Matt would then turn his red-crayoned message into a paper airplane and land it expertly on the top of my desk, causing my heart to sink and my frustrations to rise. I was stymied, as nothing I was told to do in my education courses—ignore his behavior, reward compliance, have a one-on-one meeting with Matt—worked. We had a very bad year . . . until March.

On a cold morning that could not rightfully be called spring in the northern New Hampshire town where I taught, Matt entered my classroom having just been sprayed by a skunk. It might be hard to believe, but this smelly incident changed my career and, I hope, Matt's education forever. Here's how.

Matt had been checking on his backyard "business" of maple sugar farming. Maple sap starts to flow as the days get a tad longer and warmer, and Matt was checking on the buckets attached to his sugar maples to see how much bounty he'd collected. He had signed contracts with neighbors to tap their trees in return for some of the syrup he and his dad would make from the collected sap that they distilled into sweet, liquid sugar. He was also trying (in vain) to sell his product at our town's single grocery store, but he couldn't do so without

having his syrup OK'd for quality by the state department of agriculture. The skunk came into play due to the fact that maple sugaring season also happens to be mating season for these smelly carnivores, and Matt had inadvertently waltzed between two amorous skunks that were seeking a bit of privacy.

Hence, he got sprayed.

Matt and I talked (downwind) about this incident and decided, together, that maple sugar would become a main focus of his curriculum. This was hardly something I could have planned in advance; rather, it was my desperate attempt to salvage even a bit of learning from this misbegotten school year. So, from that day forward, Matt's math assignments changed from engaging in rote drills to more relevant tasks, such as making change and converting volume amounts. Reading and writing assignments involved filling out invoices and making posters to advertise his product. A major social studies assignment evolved into a photo essay highlighting his maple sugar farming skills (complete with an original script), presented in the now-quaint carousel slide projector technology of the 1970s. Science involved talking to a mentor from the community who was an established maple sugar farmer and would help Matt gain the state department of agriculture's stamp of approval (which happened two years later). Matt even spoke at a Rotary Club luncheon where, truth be told, he listened to old war stories and contributed a tasteless joke or two to the colorful discussion. All in all, we ended our time together that year on much sounder footing than how we began.

Was Matt an underachiever prior to this maple syrup epiphany? I think not. Rather, I believe Matt was "selective"—not "turned off"—when it came to his education. What Matt needed was a reason to learn, a reason to care about school, and a purpose that went beyond what he perceived as stale textbooks. Almost like Dorothy in *The Wizard of Oz*, Matt found the magic of learning to be right in his own backyard—not a Kansas cornfield but a New Hampshire sugar maple grove called home.

Today, Matt is living in Alaska among the woods he has always loved and is more than 50 years old. Thanks to Matt, I came to appreciate early in my career that "underachievement" is a whole lot more complex than just doing poorly in school. Its foundation is something much more basic: dignity, or the lack thereof, that kids such as Matt believe is absent from this educational enterprise we call school.

In the following pages, I wish to present you with a snapshot of underachievement that may look far different from what you envision it to be. While giving you practical solutions to reach these students, I ask you to open yourself up and allow a new perspective on this perplexing problem that has dogged the lives of smart, poorly performing kids for far too long.

One logistical point: throughout this book, you will read about the experiences of various students I've had the honor and pleasure to teach or counsel. Portions of some of these student examples have appeared in a few of my previous books (especially the cases of Marty and Sierra that I present in Chapter 1), and many of the examples I use are "composites" of several students whose individual stories are rolled into one story. I have no doubt that you'll also see several of your own students through my examples and the student quotes I've included throughout.

1

Underachievement: Viewing It from a Student's Perspective

Let's begin with a quick word association. When I say *underachiever*, what other terms come to mind? My hunch is that words such as *lazy, unmotivated, bored,* and *slacker* are near the top of the list, none of which is positive. Now imagine that you are this smart kid who doesn't do well in school. Teachers, counselors, and parents all come together with collective anxiety that you are "wasting your potential" by not doing work that you are certainly capable of completing.

This is an important point. It's not that the schoolwork you are being asked to do is too challenging or difficult—in fact, it's just the opposite. The mind-numbing assignments you could finish off in minutes remain undone because you see no point in doing them. If you continue to get *A*s and *B*s on quizzes and tests—which you most often could do—then why do you have to complete homework and in-class tasks that are really designed for students who haven't yet grasped the content as well as you have? You feel like you're being punished for knowing stuff that classmates are still trying to master.

And this issue didn't just appear suddenly in middle or high school. No, the genesis of your dissatisfaction began long ago, in situations such as the following:

> In 2nd grade, I had already read the *Harry Potter* books, and circle reading in class was painful for me. "Animals live all over the world. Some places are cold while others are not. The Arctic is cold and snowy." Sentences like these just don't compare to sentences like "The two men appeared out of nowhere, a few yards apart in the narrow, moonlit lane."

But in 2nd grade (and 3rd and 4th) you likely keep much of your academic dissatisfaction to yourself. You might tell your parents and friends that school is "boring," but hey . . . everyone thinks that, right? So you continue to turn in addition and subtraction worksheets even though you've been doing complex multiplication for a year already. Spelling words such as *world* and *planet* come easily to you since you are in the midst of watching Neil deGrasse Tyson's *Cosmos* on YouTube. Needless to say, your perfect spelling tests don't matter to you at all.

So you begin to wonder, "Maybe it's me." If almost everyone else seems satisfied with the level of work he or she is being asked to complete, maybe *you're* the one who has a problem. But as your body and mind continue to mature and you enter middle school, you begin to realize that your academic desires are higher than those of many of your classmates'. You want your education to be relevant and interesting: two qualities sadly lacking in the curriculum you are expected to complete.

With that in mind, you begin to disassociate from classmates whose knowledge base is lower than yours, and you tune out most class lessons and only listen to your teachers when a topic seems intriguing or important to you personally. You long to be anywhere but in English class, and your reactions become unmistakable. That's when the anxious teachers, counselors, and parents convene on your behalf. You're told that when you finish school and begin to work, some elements of your job will be boring, too, yet they still have to be done. You think to yourself, "Yeah, but if I'm bored every day like I am now in school, I'll look for a new job." But leaving school in 7th grade? I don't think so.

The downward spiral continues, and everyone in this situation ultimately ends up frustrated. Where do you go from here? Before we get to some possible solutions, let's dissect this thing called underachievement in more detail.

Special Education of a Different Sort

Although the first book specifically targeting underachievement—*Bright Underachievers* (Raph, Goldberg, & Passow, 1966)—was published more than 50 years ago, the issue of smart students getting poor grades has certainly existed long before then. Logically speaking, it's only to be expected that when you put a diverse group of people in any learning situation, some individuals will be more skilled and attentive than others. And if modifications are made so that people are allowed—indeed, encouraged—to learn at their own pace while exploring topics of personal interest, then underachievement is not likely to be a big issue.

However, when this set of diverse learners happens to be students in a classroom where individual needs and abilities are not accommodated fully, then it's the students on the edges—those with learning difficulties and with intellectual giftedness—who most often lose out on learning at levels that are personally appropriate. To address this reality, our nation allocates billions of dollars annually to help students with disabilities and learning difficulties, hoping that adequate interventions will help them achieve at levels they might not otherwise reach. This money is both well spent and well deserved.

But money for smart students—those who score in the top 5 percent on standardized tests of achievement or aptitude—is sorely limited by comparison. Unfortunately, virtually no federal funds exist specifically for educating gifted children, and only modest state and local funds—if any—target this population. Whereas students with learning difficulties get sympathy and empathy from a generous public that wants them to do well, the most academically capable students—especially those who do poorly in school—are often told to "get over themselves" and just buckle down and do their assignments. Very little sympathy or empathy is extended to these students. Why? Because the public in general thinks that gifted students are smart and can "make it on their own."

But perhaps our dismissal of students who underachieve is misplaced, as evidenced by this quote from educational pioneer James J. Gallagher (1975):

> Failure to help the gifted child reach his potential is a societal tragedy, the extent of which is difficult to measure but which is surely great. How can we measure the sonata unwritten, the curative drug undiscovered, the absence of political insight? They are the difference between what we are and what we could be as a society. (p. 9)

Our nation and our world are not so well off that we can readily dismiss the very real needs of smart kids who do poorly in school. Just as students who underachieve may need to cut educators a little slack when it comes to making every lesson as exciting as an episode of your favorite show, so must the adults in these kids' lives be willing to listen to the legitimate issues often raised by kids who do poorly on purpose.

A Little More History

> What was unimaginable a generation ago has begun to occur—other (nations) are matching and surpassing our educational attainments. . . . If an unfriendly foreign power had attempted to impose on America the mediocre educational performance that exists today, we might very well have viewed it as an act of war. (National Commission on Excellence in Education, 1983, p. 9)

This observation, from the landmark *A Nation at Risk* report, offered a scathing indictment of much of America's educational system and practices. Among the findings specific to the topic of underachievement, the Commission found that

- More than half of identified gifted students did not match their tested ability through their school performance.
- The majority of secondary school students had mastered 80 percent of the content of their textbooks *before* ever opening them for the school year.
- School curricula, for the most part, focused on memorization and acquisition of low-level skills, not on problem solving and analysis.

Stating that American education offered a "rising tide of mediocrity" (p. 9) to its students, the Commission determined that much curricula was about a mile wide and an inch deep, barely scratching the surface of in-depth analysis that many highly capable students desire. Given this situation, one might say that underachievement is learned by many because it is taught so well in schools.

I know. I'm going to be criticized for highlighting these generation-old data, but if you presented today's underachieving students with these findings and asked them to guess when they were compiled, many might assume it was last week—not last century.

For a while, *A Nation at Risk* caused eruptions of anger and no small amount of hand wringing from politicians and educators over how to address the issues it raised. However, as often happens with government publications and initiatives, very little actual long-term progress was made. In 1995, David Berliner and Bruce Biddle actually took exception to the Commission's findings, calling them politically motivated results that engineered a manufactured crisis in education. John Goodlad (2003) disagreed with this assertion and supported the Commission's work, yet he commented that the report had plenty of smoke but no flames. And in a 25-year retrospective offered by former U.S. Secretary of Education Margaret Spellings, the U.S. Department of Education (2008) maintained that "we remain a nation at risk, but now we are a nation informed, a nation accountable, and a nation that recognizes there is much work to be done" (p. 1). You'd think that after 25 years, Spellings could have offered more specifics and fewer platitudes.

What do these findings have to do with the topic of under-achieving students who brought you to read this book in the first place? Just about everything. Indeed, smart students who do poorly on purpose may be the educational equivalent of canaries in a coal mine—students who, despite being academically capable, refuse to do schoolwork that lacks both challenge or relevance and, in doing so, are warning others to "get out fast." As averse as some educators may be to taking guidance from smart students whose academic performance is minimal, these very students may be the ones whose ideas for improving education can offer some positive paths forward.

Underachievement is more than getting lower grades than you are capable of achieving. Indeed, it is a complex issue that involves personal interpretation and nuance, as described in the rest of this book.

More Conundrum Than Consensus

My Aunt Peggy was a sweet woman, but when it came to my career decision, she was not shy about telling me that she thought I had really underplayed the cards I'd been dealt. Always a smart kid in school, I earned a PhD in educational psychology at the age of 28. I was thrilled (if tired), and my parents were equally ecstatic—I was and remain the first and only member of my extended family to receive a doctorate.

At my celebration party, Aunt Peggy sat me down and told me how proud she was of me and how much good credit I had given to our family name. Then she dropped her bombshell: "You were always a smart kid, Jimmy, so it's a shame you didn't decide to become a *real* doctor. You know, a medical doctor—the kind of doctor who really helps people."

Until the day she died, Aunt Peggy considered me an underachiever. Mind you, she had never ventured beyond high school herself, but her opinion of my doctorate was undercut by her unwillingness to consider a PhD a worthwhile degree for "a smart kid" like me.

Issue 1: Underachievement is often a phenomenon based on personal opinion rather than established norms.

Consider this: in your life as an educator (or counselor or parent) I'm sure you have known students who consider a grade of *B+* to be low, whereas another student who gets a *D–* will remind you that it's still a passing grade. So, when it comes to grades, where does underachievement stop and achievement begin? And does context matter? Is a lower grade in an honors or AP class "better" than a higher grade in a standard class? How proud should students be when they get high grades in a class where they didn't learn anything new?

These issues are often sidestepped when we discuss grades with students who are not performing academically at levels their intelligence indicates they are capable of achieving. Instead, we tell them to "try your best" or to "work up to your potential"—two statements that are banal suggestions with absolutely no specificity. Students need specificity.

Issue 2: There is no such thing as a "classic underachiever."

Every so-called underachiever with whom I have worked is good at some things that either don't get recognized or acknowledged as important by adults. Yes, they may be doing poorly in regular school classes, but ask about their National History Day project they've been working on for almost a year and you'll see eyes widen and ears perk to attention. They may be earning a *C–* in Algebra II, but the Internet business they began on their own? It's up, running, and successful.

Repeat this mantra: "no one—*no one*—is good or bad at everything." When we use the term *classic underachiever*, the presumption is that this lack of success is pervasive, not content or situation specific. Nevertheless, I would say that 99 times out of 100, underachievement is dependent on factors other than intelligence. The same student who will walk on nails for a teacher who asks, "What are you interested in learning and how can I help you achieve your goals?" will dismiss a teacher who says, "I don't care how smart you think you are, *all* of my students need to turn in their homework. Review and practice are good for you."

The word *dignity* appears in the subtitle of this book for a reason. If smart students don't feel that they are getting it from those in charge of their learning, then their desire to conform and achieve is minimized. By asking capable students to complete assignments that are several strata below their abilities, we ignore the very qualities that got them identified as intelligent in the first place. Where's the dignity in *that*?

Issue 3: Underachievement may be caused by one or more of the following: lack of interest, lack of challenge, lack of self-esteem, or a desire to receive negative attention over none at all.

A third reason why underachievement has been so hard to address successfully has to do with its genesis—its origins. In some ways, underachievement is akin to a skin rash. The symptoms may look the same on different people, yet the underlying causes of the rash (or the underachievement) might be very different. Alternatively, underachievement can be like an onion, a multitiered phenomenon with so many layers that the more you peel away, the more you find underneath. Underachievement also often appears as a labyrinth, with so many paths to go down that you don't know which ones will lead to success and which will lead to dead ends until you try multiple possibilities.

The lack of interest or challenge has already been addressed, and the low self-esteem issue will be dealt with in a later section, but the desire for negative attention over none at all is one of critical importance that is seldom addressed.

Let's go to a classic movie as an example: *The Breakfast Club*. During a weakly monitored Saturday detention at the fictitious Shermer High School, a group composed of an athlete, a "smart kid," a stoner, a rebel, and a princess reveal just how much they have in common despite their outward personae that scream "I'm different than all of you." The rebel, John Bender (played by Judd Nelson), has a dad who beats him, a false and scary bravado, and no positive relationships with any adult. Why should he? He's been written off by practically everyone as a loser, yet the desire to be included—to be somebody who matters—is as much a part of his human nature as it is for the school's most successful students. Since he can't get positive attention, he decides to get as much negative attention as he can. He'll do anything to feel relevant.

With some underachievers, their quest for relevance is not fictional but very real. Why not address it directly? Jean Peterson (2008), a school counselor and author who understands underachievers from the inside out, suggests having *"Breakfast Club*–like" discussions with teens that focus on questions such as these (p. 32):

- Where in your life are you letting your intelligence show?
- Who in your life believes you are an intelligent person?
- What is the most comfortable part of school? The least comfortable?
- What are your feelings about being labeled an 'underachiever'?
- What would happen if you started achieving in school?
- When you underachieve, who gives you attention?
- Who are you being loyal to by underachieving?
- What are you sacrificing by underachieving?

Almost more than anything else, highly able teens who do not achieve want something they frequently lack: an adult who cares about who they are, not just how well they do in school. This lack of bonding with an adult is one of the main reasons why solving the issue of underachievement is so difficult, and it will be one of the primary foci of this book.

A Few More Psychological Factors to Consider

Of course, we cannot clump all underachievers into one big pool of disappointing school performers. Some underachieve chronically, year after year, and no amount of counseling or cajoling seems to help. Other students underachieve for a very good reason (e.g., a family divorce, a move to a new school, a teenage love affair gone sour). In these instances, the underachievement is often temporary as school takes on less importance when other aspects of their lives are causing personal turmoil.

In addition, some students who could shine academically choose not to do so unless they are assured of being the top student in class. This can occur in honors or AP courses, where the level of academic rigor is high and student competition to get top grades borders on maniacal. In these situations, a student who fears getting anything less than a top grade might actually opt to put minimal effort into the workload. A resulting low grade of *C* or *D* elicits comments such as "You could have done better than this" from adults, and to this point, the student agrees. But guess what? For students expected to get *A*s, a grade of *C* might actually be safer and more satisfying, psychologically speaking, than a *B+*. In essence, it feels better (temporarily) to come closer to failure than to the success others expect you to achieve.

There is actually a term for this phenomenon: *counterfactual thinking*. It is when a person's emotional response to disappointing events is influenced by his or her thoughts about "what might have been." To wit, psychology researchers from Cornell University published a study in which they videotaped and then analyzed the facial expressions of silver and bronze medal winners at the 1992 Summer Olympics in Barcelona (Medvec, Madey, & Gilovich, 1995). Almost without fail, the bronze medal winners showed "Duchenne smiles," which is a scientific way of saying that a smile is genuine and not forced, whereas the silver medal winners had smiles that were polite but not real. Similar studies were done at the 1994 Empire State Games and the 2004 Summer Olympics in Athens with similar results: Duchenne smiles for third-place finishers and fake smiles from those winning silver.

So what's the conclusion? Those who are objectively better off in terms of success but still not the best (e.g., a silver medalist, a kid with an 89-percent average) feel worse than those who don't achieve as strongly (e.g., a bronze medalist, a student who squeaked by with an 81-percent average). Counterfactual thinking is an undiscussed reality that affects the attitude and performance of many an underachiever.

A related phenomenon can occur when highly able students get their wishes granted and are placed in classes where they are finally learning something new and being challenged. What seems like a dream come true can be, for students more afraid of academic failure than they thought they were, their biggest nightmare. Why? Because now, for maybe the first time in their academic careers, they might not be the smartest one in the class. They might not be able to ace exams without studying. They might now have the *need* to study but, because they've never had to do so before, they don't know *how* to study.

All of this can lead to something I call the "Bottom of the Top" syndrome, where students recognize that they had to be smart to enroll in a particular course but, as they look around the classroom, they believe that everyone else is going to be smarter than they are, so . . . why try at all? This self-doubt, which is generally never discussed with students, could be the catalyst for a downward spiral of grades and academic expectations. Self-sabotage (defined as behavior that creates problems and interferes with long-standing goals) is rearing its ugly head.

I've seen this situation firsthand in my part-time role as a high school teacher for highly gifted teens. Located on a college campus, this small, public school with only 200 students attracts what others call "the best and the brightest" from our county. Me? I just call them smart adolescents who need a challenge and a place to feel at home both socially and intellectually. Working primarily with incoming 9th graders, I try to help students see how they can balance academics with other life aspects (e.g., sports, band, free time with family and friends), which is a challenge for many since their freshman year is often filled with honors and AP classes and with for-credit college courses. Academic expectations are high from every direction—from their parents, from their teachers and professors, and—especially—from themselves.

During my first day with students, I distribute a 10-item check-list. "What do freshmen worry about most when starting at our school?" I ask them to complete the list anonymously.

- I will fail, so why should I even be coming here?
- I'm really not gifted, it's just a label people pin on me to get me to work hard.
- I won't find any friends who really "get" me.
- I'll have to fake who I am if I want to fit in.
- I will be bored—as usual—in my classes.
- I will feel more pressure to perform because I'm in a "gifted school."
- I've never had to study before to get good grades, so I don't know *how* to study.
- I'm going to be intimidated sitting next to college students in class.
- I'm going to be so busy with academics that I won't have time to do anything fun.
- I'm probably going to be the dumbest of the smart kids.

Once they're finished, I ask students to close their eyes as I read each statement and raise their hands for any they've identified as being of personal concern. Without fail, the statement that garners the most concern is "I'm probably going to be the dumbest of the smart kids." About 70 percent of students indicate this as a fear. With their eyes now wide open—literally and figuratively—I remind them that it is statistically impossible for 70 percent of them to be the dumbest of the smart kids, and this is the beginning of a series of discussions we have about the effect the "Bottom of the Top" syndrome can have on their success and self-esteem.

To be sure, this is not a school for students who underachieve chronically, and those few who do not succeed academically are counseled to return to their base high schools. Still, the importance of discussing the possibility of disappointing yourself or others with a "dreadful" grade (a *B+* or *C–*, depending on the student) is paramount to getting students to accept personal disappointment and vulnerability. It's also one among many reasons why raising the issue of "failure" with students and their parents makes much more sense than ignoring it.

The many possible causes of bright students performing poorly have made the issue of underachievement a puzzle that won't go away. Before going any further, let's try to separate the many varieties of underachievers into two categories, both of which you have undoubtedly seen in your classrooms, homes, or counseling offices.

Underachiever or Selective Consumer? Two Sides of a Complicated Coin

Sierra is a 5th grader who wishes she was as smart as her teachers say she is. Year after year, teachers have commented that Sierra's insecurities about her abilities really hold her back when it comes to excelling academically. A quiet girl, Sierra never causes trouble in class; in fact, above all else, she values her teachers' approval and just wants to please them—she just doesn't believe she is competent enough to do so.

Teachers have tried to persuade Sierra that she is smart by commenting positively on tests or projects where she has excelled. However, Sierra dismisses these accolades and takes no personal responsibility for her academic successes. She says, "I just got lucky, I guess." However, when Sierra does not do well on an assignment, it just reinforces her already low opinion of her abilities; she internalizes this weak performance, calls herself dumb, and shies away from future projects that she thinks will be too difficult to complete.

Sierra really does want to do better in school than her low grades indicate, but she claims she can't. Some might think that Sierra is a nice, quiet girl who just lacks confidence, but the truth is that Sierra is a sad girl who cannot seem to get beyond her own self-criticism, which is keeping her from succeeding as her teachers believe she can.

Sierra is an underachiever, right?

Marty is a 7th grader who most teachers hear about before he ever reaches their classroom door. Comments such as "He's a smart kid who always thinks he's right—watch out for him" and "He'll do great work one day and no work the next—I can't figure this kid out" pervade teacher-lounge conversations.

To be sure, teaching Marty can lead to frustration. On some days, he'll come to class and lead an animated discussion on a topic of personal interest, whereas other days he'll just sit there with an "I dare you to teach me something" look in his eyes.

Marty dislikes busywork and the teachers who assign it, and he seldom turns in homework that he could complete in no time flat. This, of course, makes assigning grades to Marty difficult, for even if he's proven that he knows the material, how can he be rewarded with high grades if he doesn't hand in basic homework assignments? It wouldn't be fair to the other, more compliant students. This situation frustrates nearly everyone—except Marty. He knows that he's smart, and he also knows he could get straight *As* if he "played school by the rules." But he honestly doesn't care about good grades; he loves to learn, but if Marty feels he is just jumping through hoops to earn them, he'd rather not play the school game by someone else's rules.

Some teachers think that Marty is rebelling for the sake of rebelling and that if he isn't willing to cut them a little slack, then they're not going to cut him any, either. A few, though, recognize that Marty is just fed up with "learning" material that he mastered long ago, so they try to meet him halfway and not get into power struggles where everyone loses.

Marty is an underachiever, right?

If you examined Sierra's and Marty's report cards, you wouldn't notice much difference; both would indicate smart students who are underperforming. However, as my mother was fond of saying, "these two are as different as chalk and cheese." Treating them the same, similar grades notwithstanding, would be a disservice to them both.

Let's now examine how Sierra and Marty—and the countless others like them—differ in both observable and unseen ways. First, let's consider the dynamics behind Sierra's lack of achievement. By her own admission, Sierra doesn't understand why she isn't performing well in school. Dependent on teacher feedback, Sierra internalizes only the negatives about her school progress. Seldom if ever confrontational, she has great respect for her teachers and feels badly that she is disappointing them. She does best when her assignments are short-term and highly structured, yet her grades vary little across subject areas. She believes she is equally bad in everything she does academically. Ironically, though, Sierra tends toward perfectionism, preferring not to turn in an assignment at all rather than risk having it be lacking in quality. This poor academic self-image has been a long-term issue for Sierra, and her teachers have met frequently with her parents and school counselors in hopes of getting this intelligent girl to appreciate, even a little, the abilities she has. So far, nothing seems to have worked for more than a short period of time.

Given these characteristics and qualities, I would label Sierra as an underachiever. The issues she confronts daily go far beyond the quality of her schoolwork, as her self-concept as a learner is extremely low and the helplessness she feels in making things better is genuine. More an issue of counseling than teaching, Sierra will require a long-term, committed strategy to avoid falling back further in subsequent years.

Then there's Marty. He'll explain to anyone who cares to listen why he is not doing well in most school subjects—the material is irrelevant or boring, and he believes most teachers are there simply to collect a paycheck. He has a definite independent streak and tends to rebel when placed in an academic setting that he finds stultifying. Teachers are his adversaries until they've been proven otherwise, but once Marty accepts a teacher as someone who listens to him and cares about what *he* cares about, he will become (for the most part) a compliant, successful student. Although Marty needs some structure, he is comfortable with more amorphous, ill-defined assignments or projects, often bringing a creative spin to his work that surprises his teachers and causes them to ask, "Why can't he *always* turn in work like this?"

Marty considers himself academically capable, yet his grades are all over the place—one year he'll earn an *A* in math, and the next year a *C* or *D*. The reason? He performs well for teachers who treat him respectfully as an intelligent person and dismisses those who don't. Perfection is seldom a part of Marty's academic repertoire, unless it is a project of his own design in which his time and talents are heavily invested. Although most teachers dread the thought of having Marty in their classrooms, a few see him as a rebel with a cause—an agent with a mission—who strives to take the best from school and leave the rest behind. Counseling has been tried sporadically but with little progress. After all, Marty *knows* what is expected of him in school; he just chooses to play by his own rules.

Marty's scenario suggests that he is not the underachiever people claim he is. Rather, Marty is a *selective consumer* who is quite picky about when he will perform academically and when he won't. To be sure, there are adults who worry that Marty will become a belligerent adult who refuses to conform to society's rules, making him incapable of taking orders, holding down a job, or being committed to any long-term personal relationships. Those who believe this about Marty want to control and contain him *now* . . . before it's too late. The trouble with this approach is that Marty refuses to buy into a system that wants *him* to do all the changing—where's the dignity in that? Instead, a less-confrontational, hands-off manner in which

Marty is presented with his options and their consequences is the type of realistic approach that is likely to do more good than harm.

Underachievers and selective consumers—chalk and cheese, indeed.

In subsequent chapters, I will address the fundamentals of dealing with both types of learners, although I will focus more attention on the students who come onto our radars pretty quickly: the Martys of the world. It is not that underachievers such as Sierra should be ignored—indeed, in the long run, her problems may go deeper and far beyond schoolwork concerns. However, selective consumers like Marty are the ones who have been lost to a school system that demands conformity and imposes punishments and contracts that never get to the heart of the issue that causes selective consumers to rebel in the first place.

I feel more sympathy for Sierra than I do for Marty, as she is as emotionally fragile as Marty is strong. However, every teacher and counselor wants to help Sierra succeed, and there is little disagreement that she needs consistent and caring guidance. On the other hand, many teachers and counselors are apt to write Marty off as a spoiled renegade if their initial attempts to get him to improve his attitude and grades fall short of success. In the long run, both Sierra and Marty need our support, just in very different ways.

Summary

Why is it that concepts that seem so obvious and clear upon first glance become less obvious and muddier the more they are examined? Such is the case with the term *underachievement*, which, when defined simplistically, refers to a student with high intellectual aptitude who performs academically far below tested abilities. The deeper you dig, though, the more you realize that this simple concept of underachievement may be precise and measurable, but it is also too narrow for those trying to help these so-called underachievers.

Ultimately, underachievement comes in many forms. A solution for one won't necessarily work for another, and even though weak academic performance seems to be the common denominator, the reasons behind students' low achievement vary considerably. Students such as Sierra crave teacher support and guidance, whereas students such as Marty often shun both. Sierra will be the first to point out how poor a student she is, but Marty will pity the teachers who aren't bright enough to realize just how smart *he* really is. Sierra dismisses any comment from adults that focuses on her strengths and sporadic high academic performance, yet Marty will be happy to let you know that the low grades he earns in class are justified, given the lame assignments he is expected to complete.

In unique ways, both Sierra and Marty feel like victims. Sierra is a victim of her own poor self-concept as a learner, which prevents her from doing a level of work that teachers believe she is competent of performing. Marty feels victimized by not receiving the credit he deserves—the *dignity* he deserves—to have his many strengths acknowledged even when he doesn't complete his teachers' most basic assignments.

The search for solutions for both Sierra and Marty will be filled with as many pitfalls as triumphs, yet if the end result is that these two very different types of underachievers start to succeed on both their own terms and those of their teachers, then the efforts we make to help them will be worth the long trek down a path that is often unclear.

Let the journey for solutions begin.

2

A Little Light Research

Instead of taking the expected route and beginning this book with an overview of the research on underachievement, I chose to introduce you to some kids who have entered my life and fit into the two categories of *underachievers* and *selective consumers*. The research on underachievement is quite extensive yet much of it (in my opinion) is not very useful. Nevertheless, it is still incumbent upon me to review the theoretical bases for this field of study. I think you'll find that, with one notable exception, there have been lots of studies but very few definitive conclusions. With that in mind, let's begin by stepping back in time.

The *Sputnik* Effect

We have the Russians to thank for our nation's emphasis on underachievement. When they launched *Sputnik* in 1957, Americans went into full panic mode, fearing we were going to come up short against the Russians in everything scientific. Frantic attempts were made to improve math and science education in America's schools, and gifted kids were identified in droves and sent to special schools or programs that would focus on what we now call STEM subjects—science, technology, engineering, and mathematics (Jolly, 2009).

Some kids did great in these programs; others did not. Obviously, factors other than raw intelligence played into a gifted student's success. Factors such as personality, motivation, peer relations, and parental involvement were soon used to help determine how we could get the most kids to succeed. Today, it seems obvious that students' performance in school and academic success include these non-intellective factors but, up until the late 1950s, they were seldom considered.

Since the magnitude of the problem had not been investigated thoroughly, estimates of the number of underachievers among gifted students ranged wildly, from 15 percent (Strang, 1960) to 50 percent (Hildreth, 1966). In one bizarrely titled book, *Able Misfits: A Study of Educational and Behavior Difficulties of 103 Very Intelligent Children (IQs 120–200)* (Pringle, 1970), the author contended that gifted underachievers weren't initially identified from their school performance but only when other types of "problem children" were being investigated—including an appreciable number of juvenile delinquents (Pringle's term)—who showed a marked discrepancy between their intellectual aptitude and relatively low academic achievement.

Whereas Pringle saw the problem of underachievement as one limited to a small number of individuals, Benjamin Fine (1967) put a rather existential spin on the topic, writing that, "We are almost all of us, underachievers. . . . We are not living in a time or in a society that demands total performance. . . . Almost all of us are specialists, and are not expected to perform to the maximum of our abilities in more than a few limited areas" (pp. 233–234).

This brief review of early studies of underachievement reveals the confusion about both identifying and "fixing" the problem that goes back decades. In fact, about the only source of agreement that seems to exist among early researchers of this topic is one of timing. Although underachievement appears to be an issue with adolescents, the seeds of academic discomfort are sown at a much younger age. As summarized by Whitmore (1980),

> It is disturbing to realize that studies of fourth graders reveal the same factors as have been found with high school and college underachievers, suggesting that the pattern associated with underachievement is fairly well established by the fourth grade at least and apparently persists and increases over the years of schooling. . . . Therefore, underachievement can be viewed as a social product, not just the problem of the child. (p. 194)

As is true in so many other educational venues, early intervention seems to be key to addressing the issue of underachievement. It just took a few decades for researchers to figure that out.

Back to history. Once the *Sputnik* scare was over and the United States was well on its way to the first moon landing, interest in gifted students waned as quickly as it had waxed. Fifteen years after *Sputnik* was launched, intensive programs specifically for gifted students were few and far between. Indeed, they were overtaken by America's new focus: identifying and serving children from poverty and minority groups who struggled to achieve academically, as well as a large-scale focus on children with disabilities. Given these new national educational priorities, the emphasis on smart kids who did poorly in school was no longer the focus it had once been. It became relegated to an asterisk in the history of educational reform.

Until 1980.

Enter Joanne Rand Whitmore:
The Underachieving Student's Best Friend

Earlier, I mentioned one notable exception in the field of under-achievement that eclipses all other research, before or since. That plaudit goes to Joanne Rand Whitmore, whose 1980 book *Giftedness, Conflict, and Underachievement* remains the most careful analysis of this topic ever completed.

Here's some background. Whitmore was a teacher employed in the highly affluent Cupertino Union Elementary District (CUED) in what is now known as Silicon Valley, California. This school district, a breath away from Stanford University, was filled with successful, smart adults whose children were also smart and destined for success. At least that was the plan.

As a primary school teacher, Whitmore noticed that gifted underachievers were summarily excluded from the special gifted classes that did exist in CUED and were instead relegated to hetero-geneously grouped settings with students who performed well below grade level. Intelligent children with hostile or disruptive behaviors were often sent for psychological testing, which frequently resulted in labels of *behaviorally disordered* or *educationally handicapped* and subsequent placement in special classes where the emphasis was on conformity—not challenge and academic excellence. When the CUED administrators noticed this situation, they decided to imple-ment the Cupertino Program for Highly Gifted Underachievers, an experimental program that "established self-contained classes for students who evidenced need of an intensive program of social and emotional rehabilitation as well as academic remediation" (Whit-more, 1980, p. 206). And Joanne Whitmore was selected to be one of the program's teachers.

The rationale for the design of this program was that if all of the students who had been identified as dysfunctional in their regular or gifted classes were bunched together, then their patterns of severe and chronic underachievement could be attended to directly and frequently, thereby resulting in improved behavior and enhanced academic performance. The initial expectation was that primary-age students would need one year in this placement and inter-mediate-grade students would likely need two years in this special program.

Whitmore mentioned a number of particular beliefs undergird-ing the need for this type of program.

Children needed to decrease invidious comparisons with high achievers. In CUED's regular gifted classes, 2nd graders often performed at the 7th and 8th grade levels on standardized tests and were often labeled as *omnibus gifted kids*—in other words, they were good at everything they tried to do. This excellence often intimidated the underachievers, who typically performed at or below grade level.

Children needed to develop self-acceptance through accep-tance of others with similar problems. More than just an academic environment, these special classes included extensive sharing through guided discussions. By reviewing topics such as feelings of failure and rejection and the frustration of being smart while lacking some basic learning skills, it was hoped that students would gain both self-accep-tance and the ability to help others cope with similar struggles.

Children needed to enjoy rewarding intellectual stimula-tion and a curriculum centered on their strengths and past suc-cess. Highly developed verbal communication and thinking skills were what brought these kids to the attention of adults in the first place, so these skills were emphasized in the classroom. Rote learn-ing was kept to a minimum, and a focus on hands-on activities in sci-ence, social studies, and the arts took priority.

Children needed to acquire a sense of genuine success. Getting the highest grade in a low-level class seldom brought any sense of satisfaction to these students, so challenging activities were designed instead. Debate, independent research, scientific experimentation, and creative productivity in the arts with classmates who shared similar high abilities were all part of the daily agenda.

Children needed to develop social skills and the potential for leadership. In their other classes, these underachieving students were seen as "problem kids," both by their teachers and classmates who seldom looked to them for advice or leadership. In this self-contained environment, though, it was believed that their perceptiveness and sensitivity—two traits very common among gifted children—would better allow them to minister to their own needs and the needs of others.

Kids weren't just shuttled from one classroom to another, year after year, with academic benchmarks being the *sine qua non* of success. Instead, with a focus on what we now call soft skills—self-awareness, awareness of others, empathy, compassion, and the ability to listen—these underachieving students found a classroom that truly resembled a home. Indeed, this approach to education might rightly be described as resembling a family more than a factory.

A total of 29 students comprised the class, which ran from 1968–1970. As predicted, most kids stayed for only one or two years, with only four students remaining involved for the entire three-year period. Whitmore made this experimental class the basis of her dissertation, and she analyzed the program's success from multiple vantage points, including attendance at and participation in school, work habits, academic success, social behavior, and self-perception. In addition, she conducted formal follow-up studies of these students in 1972 and 1975 and a less-formal follow-up each year from 1976–1978.

Giftedness, Conflict, and Underachievement presents a full review of the curriculum offered to these students, a thorough analysis of the data collected over multiple years, and elaborate case studies of four of the students who participated in this experimental class. Indeed, that book deserves a thorough reading by anyone who is concerned about reversing patterns of underachievement.

So, was this experimental program successful? Whitmore says it best:

> Follow-up studies have revealed a significant number of high achievers who were evidencing leadership qualities to some extent, a slightly larger number who were inconsistent in academic achievement because of sensitive motivational factors, and a small number who were not achieving at all commensurate with their abilities and still were experiencing some intense social alienation.
>
> One interesting observation is that a disproportionate number of students are planning to enter fields of drama or music. . . . One wonders if the arts . . . have been attractive to these students because of their sense of success in those fields and the lack of appropriate academic motivation and rewarding curricula. Some of the program graduates regard themselves as "academically lazy." (Whitmore, 1980, pp. 390–391)

A point of personal privilege: I met Joanne Whitmore when I was beginning my PhD program and she had just published *Giftedness, Conflict, and Underachievement*. Within three years, she had become Dean at Kent State University's College of Education and, at her urging, I became a professor there as well, focusing for 25 years on gifted children and their well-being. In one of our many conversations about CUED's experimental program, I asked Joanne if she had one evaluative piece of data she found more telling than others. She didn't even hesitate. One of her students, a 4th grader named Tommy, was interviewed by Whitmore after spending 1st and 2nd grade in her program. When asked if he noticed a difference in himself after participating in the program, Tommy responded, "When I think of who I was in 1st grade, my eyes get wet."

Research on gifted underachievers seldom ends with perfect results, and Whitmore's monumental experiment is no exception. People are people, and their complexity demands that multiple avenues be explored in order for them to grasp the totality of who they are and who they might become. However, in the annals of underachievement research, there is no better example of striving for success than Whitmore's study of 29 children lucky enough to be in her care when they needed her most.

And Then There Are the Others Who Studied Academic Underachievement

As mentioned in Chapter 1, research on underachievement began in earnest during the 1960s, although there were some earlier, scattered attempts to address this syndrome. In a review of more than 90 research studies published between 1931 and 1961, Raph and Tannenbaum (1961) came to the particularly inconclusive conclusion that there is no unified explanation for underachievement. Similarly, Asbury (1974) determined that there were no specific psychosocial factors consistently associated with underachievement in young children.

It is hard enough to hit a target when you know where to aim, so it becomes even more difficult when that target is as elusive as determining the primary causes of underachievement. Decades later, we're still trying to identify shared traits among underachieving children. Barbara Clark (2013), a prominent advocate for gifted children, highlighted 16 such characteristics, including these:

- They have low self-concepts, as noted in their attitudes of distrust and lack of concern for or hostility toward others.

- They harbor feelings of rejection, believing that no one likes them and their parents are dissatisfied with them.
- They often leave schoolwork incomplete and sleep during study halls.
- They do not see the connection between personal effort and achievement outcomes.
- They lack study skills and have little motivation for academic tasks.
- They dislike school and teachers and choose friends who share similar feelings.
- They have immature social skills.
- They have low expectations for their own futures.
- They have a lack of intense interest in almost any topic.

When looking at Clark's entire list, it becomes clear that she has not distinguished between underachievers and selective consumers and has instead grouped all underperforming students into the same cauldron of academic discontent. In the previous chapter, I described the academic and behavioral distinctions between selective consumers and underachievers, and it's clear that Clark's characteristics need to be refined further if we are to aid and support those students who do poorly on purpose *and* those whose low school performance stems from more deeply seated issues of psychological health.

Sylvia Rimm, a prominent psychologist who has published dozens of books and articles on underachievement, parenting, and related topics, is well known for her pithy approach to identifying underachievers and reversing their downward spirals of achievement. In *Why Bright Kids Get Poor Grades and What You Can Do About It* (2008), Rimm introduces us to categorized groups of children who, depending on your point of view, are either accurate descriptions of kids you know or exaggerated versions of kids who simply don't exist:

- Dependent Conformers (e.g., Passive Paul and Perfectionistic Pearl)

- Dependent Non-Conformers (e.g., Depressed Donna and Sick Sam)
- Dominant Conformers (e.g., Social Shaundra and Dramatic Dan)
- Dominant Non-Conformers (e.g., Manipulative Maria and Bully Bob)

Through Rimm's Trifocal Model for Reversing Underachievement Syndrome, parents, educators, and underachieving students combine forces to leave behind these dependent and dominant categories and enter an inner circle of achievers. Some of her suggestions are simple common sense: parents must send united messages to their underachieving children, teachers should work to become students' allies, and students must be willing to try out suggestions presented by the adults in their lives.

Though Rimm's books and ideas have gained wide acceptability by many, I find some omissions in much of her advice, especially these two qualities: personalization and dignity. How? I find that personalization is lacking with the clustering of all children who underachieve into a finite selection of categories, and the dignity of treating each child as an individual is replaced, instead, with a boilerplate set of suggestions that may not apply to a particular child. Thus, by stipulating which strategies will work with Manipulative Maria but not with Passive Paul, Rimm groups kids together categorically in ways that strip away their individuality and the dignity that accompanies such individual recognition. Without knowing the children in question, the pronouncements of what to do with the alliterative caricatures Rimm portrays is too broad a brush with which to paint. In essence, it is hard to say that a particular strategy is unique to a student when we are trying to determine if he or she more resembles Manipulative Maria or Passive Paul. (Can't *both* kids share some common traits?)

This lack of personalization and dignity is also noticeable in another element of Rimm's work as it relates to who is ultimately

responsible for reversing underachieving behavior. Citing communication among all parties as a necessary prerequisite to reaching achievement outcomes, Rimm believes that the person most
responsible for change is the child. In her work, there is seldom any
indication that there are times when the child is right—that school
is irrelevant or homework *is* unnecessary. And if previous studies
are accurate, the tried-and-true methods of reversing patterns of
underachievement by requiring students to do all of the conforming
to adult expectations will ultimately fail, even if they may work in
the short term. Of course, children who underachieve or do poorly
on purpose have to have some skin in the game when it comes to
improving their academic performance, but to lay the entire responsibility to change on them lacks the very dignity that these children
so often seek.

The children we label as underachievers need something more
than the same old remedies that seldom cure anything. Though some
underachievers have nearly total control over their academic performance (think back to Marty, the selective consumer), others lack the
self-confidence or self-regulation to make changes by themselves
(kids such as Sierra come to mind). Some underachievers need
targeted strategies that build their self-esteem as the catalyst for
improving their schoolwork, but others need space to explore topics
of their own construction. And while kids such as Sierra may need
long-term interventions of the type that Joanne Whitmore offered
in Cupertino, kids such as Marty may perform best with teachers
who see in those students a younger version of themselves.

Frankly, research on underachievement is extremely variable when it comes to showing significant, long-term changes or
improvements in the lives of students. I harbor no illusion that the
suggestions to follow in subsequent chapters will work with every
student who brought you to this book in the first place. However, I
can promise that if we start by respecting a student's dignity as the
baseline for addressing the topic of underachievement, our chances
of success are better than if we ignored that most basic human need.

Summary

Authors who focus on underachievers have taken wildly different tacks when describing these kids, from Pringle's pejorative *able misfits* to Whitmore's more therapeutic notion that underachievers are often fragile children who need caressing over condescension. Some (like Whitmore) prefer to see each underachieving child as a unique entity, whereas Rimm offers a variety of representative characters that serve more as stereotypes than as examples of real kids.

All of these researchers, though, share one thing in common: a desire to help these capable children become more successful in school. Although some believe that a "tough love" approach of denying privileges to underachievers until they learn to cooperate and become compliant is the best strategy to pursue, others advocate for a gentler approach where underachievers' intelligence is acknowledged, their fears of failure are noted as legitimate, and their dignity is maintained by listening to their opinions on how school can be made more personally fulfilling.

It's often stated that the definition of *insanity* is doing the same thing over and over again and expecting different results. Those who wish to help underachievers become more successful in school should heed the truth of this statement and refrain from doing what has not worked for several decades: punishing kids who underachieve in the hopes that they transform into model students in response to our insistence that they toe the line academically.

Let's move on to the next chapter, where underachievement is viewed from a different perspective—that of the child who has "earned" this label.

3

Getting to *A*: Autonomy

dignity: the state or quality of being worthy of honor or respect; a sense of pride in oneself

Interesting, is it not, that dignity can be noted from both an external and internal source? Others can help us achieve it . . . or we can find it within ourselves if we dig deeply enough.

In my four decades of work with students of high ability who do not do well in school, I have learned (through *much* trial and error) that the most important asset a teacher can bring to any relationship with such students is a good set of ears. Prone as some educators can be to endless talk, it is rare to find teachers who listen more than they speak. Yet to students who do not believe that adults see their ideas or opinions as valid—I'm speaking here of selective consumers—the most important factor that prompts eventual academic success is an invitation such as "Please tell me something about yourself that most teachers don't know."

No doubt, the first time you ask a student a question like this, you are likely to be met with a blank stare and an awkward silence as he or she ponders an unstated thought: "Why do you care?" I saw this happen in a workshop I was doing with middle school students about taking charge of your education. I went around the room of 30 young adolescents, asking if any of them had thought about a career direction they might pursue. I got the usual responses of doctor, lawyer, professional athlete, and "I have no idea," but one girl, Sumiko, went into considerable detail about her dream job (to become a makeup artist for zombie apocalypse movies). There were a few titters of laughter from other students, but I just moved on and listened to the rest of the participants' responses.

During a break in the workshop, I approached Sumiko and asked her to tell me what attracted her to this potential profession. She looked at me quizzically and, after a few seconds, said just one word: "Seriously?"

"Yeah," I responded, "*Shaun of the Dead* is my favorite zombie movie *ever*, and I'm amazed at the skill it takes to make so many live actors look so dead."

For the next 10 minutes, Sumiko explained in great detail why this job was ideal for her. It involved creativity, imagination, and a refined talent to bring out the physical worst in people. When I thanked her for talking with me, Sumiko came back at me with her own thank you: "You know, every other adult I've mentioned this to tells me that a job like that is stupid and a waste of my talents. You're the only adult who's ever taken me seriously."

When you're 13 and thinking about your life as an employed adult, you seldom consider a salary, 401(k), or what status your ideal profession holds in the eyes of the world. Instead, you go right to the core: Is this job interesting, fun, and worth my time? By simply listening instead of lecturing, we give young people a chance to shine in their own light, not in a reflection of the one surrounding us.

The lesson here is that with all students, but especially with those who are prone to view traditional education with suspicion, listening 75 percent of the time and talking the other 25 percent is a proportion toward which educators should strive.

So What?

Ah yes, the quintessential question. Why does it matter that we listen to students whose academic and life goals may not match our own for them? When it comes to underachievers and selective consumers, the answer (at least to me) is obvious: *because it's seldom been done.*

In this and subsequent chapters, I'll address this issue through a variety of techniques and strategies whose theme is Getting to *A*. The *A* designation may seem to be a letter grade that indicates excellence, and should this occur with the students who are the focus of this book, I'd be thrilled. But the deeper meaning of Getting to *A* is an appreciation of the various ways we can accommodate our styles and strategies to allow students to experience success—academic and otherwise—on their own terms.

Here's what this entails:

Autonomy: How can we help our students engage and become the "masters of their universe" with respect to what education is and what it might become?

Access: How do we work with students to identify curricular challenges that are both meaningful and interesting?

Advocacy: How can we guide students toward becoming an advocate for their own education and empower them to become their own best spokesperson?

Alternatives: What new-horizon options (e.g., home school, independent study, online courses) might be appropriate with students for whom traditional school is a bad fit?

Aspirations: How can we acknowledge and respect our students' dreams and help them to achieve their personal goals?

Approachable Educators: What personal and professional dispositions can we display that invite our students to want to learn?

You may quibble that one or more of the strategies I present is misplaced. Perhaps you see one as an aspiration rather than an alternative. This could easily be true. As with many things, one person's interpretation of an event or situation differs from another's. That doesn't mean that one is right and the other is wrong; it's merely that we each use our own personal lenses to view life's daily happenings. Please don't get bogged down in "what fits where." Frankly, if a strategy works for a particular student, feel free to call it whatever you want.

That's the path ahead for the rest of this book—Getting to *A* from a variety of vantage points. Some of my suggestions will likely hit home more than others, so don't feel the need to add every single one of them to your personal repertoire of teaching strategies. Just as the students who inhabit your school are different in countless ways, so too are the adults in their lives who serve as advocates.

There is a difference between motivating us to learn and just trying to get us to improve our standardized test scores.

In too many instances, relationships between underachieving students and the meaningful adults in their lives become contentious.

There is a natural frustration, as a teacher or parent, when you have a smart student who opts not to perform well academically. However, there is *another* natural—an inclination, as an individual, to want to be given credit for your beliefs, opinions, and choices. The problem is, most adults only want to give students this form of autonomy once they start completing the level of work they are capable of doing. No one gets dessert until the Brussels sprouts are eaten, right?

If you follow this vegetables-before-ice cream path with a selective consumer, then you are likely to be one of the many who, since 1931, thought this was the best approach to use. You are also likely to fail. Further, if you try this approach with underachievers who already feel pretty lousy about themselves as both learners and people, then you are helping to dig their holes of self-loathing even deeper.

So let's try another path. Let's help these students become more autonomous, which can begin with a little dose of Psychology 101. By teaching them about some psychological constructs that are often the basis of their decision making, your students will become more aware of the reasons behind the behavioral choices they make and may become more willing to comply with adults who are actually trying to help.

Autonomy Strategy 1: Introduce the Idea of Locus of Control

The construct of locus of control was proposed in 1954 by Julian Rotter and has been a topic of interest for psychologists ever since (Rotter, 1990). It's time it *also* became of interest to educators. Basically, locus of control is an individual's interpretation of what causes and controls the events in one's life. Is everything that happens to you due to fate, luck, or other external forces beyond your control, or do you, as an individual, have some role in determining what happens to you?

Rotter subdivides locus of control into several categories. For example, some people take full credit for the positive things that happen to them (internal locus of control for success) while attributing the negatives in their lives to outside forces (external locus of control for failure). You may get annoyed when you hang around people like this, as they often appear to be braggarts who dismiss any mistakes in their lives as somebody else's fault. Then there are individuals who never give themselves credit for the good things that happen to them (external locus of control for success) while internalizing anything that didn't go right (internal locus of control for failure). You may not like hanging around with these people either, as a black cloud of despair is often looming over their heads. Some people don't distinguish between successes and failures at all—they internalize or externalize everything—but most people are a combination platter of internalization and externalization, often dependent on the context of the event in question. For example, you might internalize a lousy algebra grade by admitting to yourself that you didn't study, whereas you could externalize the same lousy grade if you pulled an all-nighter and *still* failed magnificently, saying something like "the teacher didn't give us an adequate study guide" (which could actually be true).

> If it's the first day of class and a teacher tells you how hard the class is going to be and the look on her face says, "I don't care if you pass or fail," I won't care, either. Teachers should emotionally touch their students so we know they care.

The locus of control construct becomes important when working with gifted students, many of whom easily achieve school success because the curriculum is so basic, leading them to believe they are really, really smart and will never have to lift an intellectual finger to get high grades. However, when things begin to get challenging academically, that's when the psychological fork in the road appears. Do you think to yourself, as a gifted student, "Geez . . . I've got to learn how to study if I want to continue to excel" (internal locus of control), or do you blame the "stupid teachers and their stupid lessons" for your lack of continuing success (external locus of control), as Sayler states?

> Gifted children with an internal locus of control are more likely to take responsibility for their actions and inactions. They are not easily swayed by the negative or overtly positive opinions of others. . . . Gifted children with an external locus of control may feel helpless without the concrete direction of others. They may also blame their teachers, parents, other students, or events and circumstances outside of themselves for their poor performance. (Sayler, 2009, p. 541)

Although it's logical to want to attribute an internal locus of control as "good" and an external locus of control as "bad," it's not as simple as that. In fact, for most people, the balance between the two extremes is how we live our lives. Admit it: some things, good and bad, happen by chance (e.g., winning the lottery, getting t-boned at a busy intersection), whereas other things happen because we either did or didn't prepare for them (e.g., the previous algebra test example).

Introducing students who underachieve or are selective consumers to the concept of locus of control is easy. Have them complete the 13-item, forced-choice questionnaire developed by Rotter (1966)—which is available at www.psych.uncc.edu/pagoolka/ LC.html—as a prelude to discussing how this fits into their lives. Because it does.

Often, self-knowledge is enhanced when we begin to understand that there are reasons behind the things we do and the events that happen to us. What curious student doesn't like getting into his or her own head to discover that there is some rhyme and reason to the events that define daily life? Introducing the locus of control construct to students who don't perform well in school might just be an important piece of the puzzle we call underachievement.

Autonomy Strategy 2: Introduce the Distinction between Risk-Taking and Risk-Making

Students such as our exemplar underachiever, Sierra, are often risk-averse. Believing that they are not going to do well anyway, why would they put their already fragile self-concepts on the line and try something new? Whether it is an academic task, trying out for a sports team, or even introducing themselves to someone at school who could become a good friend, underachievers frequently would rather live with the tedium of what they are experiencing now than take a chance of venturing into a new direction they believe will probably end in disappointment.

"Take a risk," we admonish these students. "What've you got to lose? You'll never win if you don't try." Statements such as this do nothing to convince the child or adolescent who worries about failing or not fitting in that the risk is worth it. However, maybe—just maybe—if it were *their* idea to push forward into a new direction, the willingness to do so might increase, even a little. That's where the distinction between risk-*taking* and risk-*making* comes into play.

Here's the distinction. When you *take* a risk, the word *take* implies that it was given to you by someone else—a teacher, coach, or parent who believes in you and wants to see you become both happy and successful. The risk you are being asked to take, therefore, comes from an external someone. However, when you *make* a risk, the person most involved in deciding to pursue something new is you. Your own "Why not?" attitude is pushing you forward; it's an internal drive to challenge yourself for your own benefit.

Underachievers are almost always more comfortable making a risk rather than taking one. Here's why. When you take a risk suggested by someone else, the person who is affected most by your performance is the individual who challenged you to take the risk in the first place. As an underachiever, you may feel good if your risk succeeds, but you still can't take full credit for your effort; the risk you took was offered by someone else. Likewise, if the risk you took doesn't pay off, then you feel a sense of guilt because you've disappointed someone who urged you to take the risk.

Contrast this scenario with one of making a risk of your own design. If the risk you make pans out, then you gain a sense of personal pride in your ability to succeed with future risks. If the risk you make for yourself doesn't pan out, then the primary person you've disappointed is yourself, which still stings but not half as much as the sting of disappointing an adult who believed in you.

Every time underachievers venture in a new direction, they are putting their "smartness" or personal pride on the line; after all, success cannot be assured. The concept of risk-making actually provides underachievers with a sense of psychological safety, which puts them more in charge of their own destiny than taking a risk from someone else ever could.

The best way to get underachievers to understand this risk-taking versus risk-making distinction is simply to explain it to them. Consider the following questions:

- Can you recall a time when you made a risk and it turned out OK (or not)? How did that make you feel?
- How did making your own risk feel compared to taking one from someone else?
- Whether the risk you made worked out or not, did it give you encouragement to make other risks in the future?

Risk-taking is akin to being pushed by someone else ("Wouldn't you like to try an advanced math course?"), whereas risk-making is you pulling yourself in a new direction ("I've always wanted to be in a school play. I think I'll audition."). This is not to imply that risk-making is superior to risk-taking, as both can be beneficial in a person's quest for self-improvement. However, for underachievers whose fear of disappointing others is extreme, the concept of risk-making may be a comfort. Furthermore, if practiced frequently enough, risk-making may give the type of ego boost that underachievers desperately need. Success seldom happens in leaps and bounds but rather in small steps. So when someone who used to hit 10 sour notes on the saxophone now hits only three of them, that's a noteworthy improvement (excuse the pun) and should be regarded as such.

A variable more likely to be important in the lives of underachievers than selective consumers, the risk-taking/making dichotomy is not the only factor influencing whether an individual wishes to try something new or different. Still, it is one more item in the psychological toolbox that helps us better understand an underachiever's willingness—or unwillingness—to move forward.

Autonomy Strategy 3: Introduce the Distinction between Self-Image and Self-Esteem

Another dichotomy that is seldom explained to students is the important distinction between two terms that are often (and erroneously) used interchangeably: *self-image* and *self-esteem*. Let's examine the difference and its importance in the lives of students who underachieve or do poorly on purpose.

Let's begin with an analogy. If you can't distinguish between a Wagyu steak and ground chuck, then your self-image as a gourmand is probably pretty bad. Likewise, if your spelling skills are so poor that you have been banished from playing Scrabble by your family, then your self-image as a wordsmith might be week . . . I mean *weak*.

But, if you don't eat red meat, you probably don't lose sleep over the fact that you'll never become a renowned carnivore, and if you think Scrabble is a game for weenies who want to show off a skill you chose not to master, then you probably shrug off game night at home and head straight for the TV.

These examples point directly to the distinction between self-image and self-esteem, as described here (Galbraith & Delisle, 2015):

- Self-image: Your perception of your ability to do a certain task, such as cook a meal, write a term paper, or make a friend.
- Self-esteem: The importance you place on your ability (or inability) to cook a meal, write a term paper, or make a friend.

"Even if your self-image as a mathematician is lower than absolute zero, this might not impact your self-esteem in the least. However, if your self-image for doing math is low and it's important to you to do well in math, your self-esteem could be negatively affected" (p. 117).

This distinction is an important one to recognize and in the case of students who underachieve (especially those who do poorly on purpose), it might help them understand some of the reasons behind their actions or inactions. For instance, why would a student take the time to complete and turn in homework perceived as worthless? A resulting grade of *F* or *A* would be seen as equally insignificant since the work that earned the student that grade was deemed purposeless. Likewise, if a school counselor sees a kid sitting alone at lunch and tries to coax him or her to engage with classmates, this prodding will fall on deaf ears if the student is genuinely not interested in making banter with others.

Teachers always tell students to "just be themselves," no matter what. They need to follow their own advice and give us the best of themselves that they have to offer.

More than anything else, this is a "skin-in-the-game" issue, for if I'm not invested in a particular task, then why should I care to do it at all? My self-esteem will not be harmed in the least by my inactions or poor performance. Therefore, until and unless adults recognize that these behaviors (or lack thereof) are based, in part, on the correlation between self-image and self-esteem, the conditions that cause underachievers to come to our attention in the first place will likely continue.

When a smart student who does poorly says, "I don't care about X," that should be the beginning of a conversation, not an ending. Every selective consumer with whom I've ever worked is good at and passionate about something. Often, though, these talents relate to activities outside of school, such as snowboarding, making music, and illustrating graphic novels. Ironically, these are the very things that are taken away until the student begins working "up to potential."

Instead of focusing on what students are not doing or performing minimally, why not locate those areas where their self-esteem is enhanced by participating in them? In doing so, we take the path toward dignity, not denigration. When we take the time to truly listen to underachievers' personal goals rather than trying to coerce them to adopt our own, we are acknowledging that they have ideals, dreams, and ambitions. Yes, we want our students to have some skin in the game when it comes to their school success, but isn't it equally important for us to put some of *our* skin in *their* game?

As I mentioned in Chapter 1, I don't believe there is such a thing as a classic underachiever. However, more times than I can count, I have heard parents and educators use that term to describe a particular student. There isn't a concrete definition for what this term actually means, but it's surely not meant as a positive descriptor. Imagine, instead, if these same students were recognized for something positive, something they love, something they've perfected or are on the path to perfecting. Little by little, changes in behaviors and attitudes might take place—in both students and the adults concerned about them.

As I've emphasized throughout this book, underachievement is not a single, all-encompassing condition, and neither is self-esteem. In fact, stating that a particular student has "low self-esteem" is a statement that is akin to calling him or her a classic underachiever. Both are terms so amorphous as to be meaningless. Unless we take context into account, we're painting such students with a brush that is far too broad to be purposeful.

If this distinction between self-image and self-esteem makes sense to you, I ask you to share it with your students. Begin the conversation by asking them to talk about something they enjoy doing and why it brings them satisfaction. Often, these will be independent tasks of their own design, where they know best when they've done well and when they haven't. Then have them tell you about something they don't enjoy doing and the reasons behind this attitude. Usually, you'll hear about an academic task that is either repetitive or irrelevant to them. If you continue the conversation and keep talking about what makes one activity worthwhile and another banal, you'll likely get to the word that is the focus of this chapter: *autonomy*. When respect for students' autonomy serves as the foundation for our efforts on their behalf, there will be far more winners than losers.

Of course we want students who underachieve to buy into some of our goals for them even if they believe them to be unimportant. However, this must not be the starting point for our efforts. Rather, it should be a long-term goal that will best be met if we initially buy into their personal ambitions and preferences. If this attention is genuine (and it will be readily evident if not), then it might be the beginning of a whole new dynamic—one where students who perform poorly on purpose and the adults in their lives actually begin moving forward together, not separately.

Summary

More than anything else, children and adolescents want to be taken seriously by the adults in their lives. They want their dreams to be respected, their voices to be heard, and their fears to be acknowledged. In other words, all students, including those who underachieve, want to feel a sense of autonomy. Even a 12-year-old has had life experiences that should matter to us.

Alex is an example of a boy who struggled mightily to convince his teachers that his voice was worth listening to. A smart, opinionated, and boisterous 6th grader, Alex was introduced to me by his school counselor. Thirty seconds into her introduction, Alex interrupted, pointing a finger in the counselor's face while looking at me: "If I'm screwed up," Alex shouted, "it's all because of her."

After a few awkward seconds, the composed counselor spoke to Alex. "Dr. Delisle is new to our school, and I thought he'd be a good person for you to get to know. Please be respectful."

Alex eyed me suspiciously. He had no reason to let me, a stranger, into his life. The counselor excused herself, and Alex and I walked to the media center to talk. I broke the silence by simply stating that I was in his school one day a week and that I would like to offer a proposition. "Your counselor must've seen something in the two of us that she thought we had in common. If you're willing to meet with me, perhaps over lunch, we can see if she was right."

Alex agreed to meet with me the following week, and I offered him this pronouncement: I would have no agenda other than getting to know him, and in case our conversations went nowhere, I'd bring along a deck of cards and we'd play poker.

The following Wednesday, Alex appeared with his lunch tray in my classroom, and I began by mentioning that I was not here to "fix" him because I didn't even know if he was broken. He smiled a wry grin, and our conversation began. Our format was this: I got to ask him one question, and he got to do the same with me—verbal ping pong, if you will. Twenty-two minutes later, we were still talking; we didn't play poker at all.

This arrangement continued for the remainder of the school year and, indeed, for the following two. We shared jokes and stories of friends and family, and at times, our talks got serious, such as when Alex shared that he had obsessive-compulsive disorder (OCD) and some social anxiety issues. Never once did that deck of cards get opened.

As 8th grade ended and my time with Alex came to a close, he arrived at my classroom with a gift: a framed poem of thanks he had written himself. We reminisced about our times together and laughed at how awkward an introduction we had to each other three years earlier.

"You know, Alex," I tapped the unopened deck of cards, "in all the times we got together, we never needed these; we always had something to talk about."

Alex laughed so hard that he spit milk out of his nose. After a few moments, he revealed his secret. "The truth is, Dr. D., I'm really, really bad at poker, so as I was coming to your classroom every week, I would think to myself, 'What can we talk about today so we won't have to play cards?'"

Alex's personality didn't change much; he remained boisterous and opinionated. Nevertheless, he had some mellowing around the edges, and he had a few teachers who loved to engage him in talks about politics. In addition, his grades and attitude steadily improved over time.

Alex is now married with a young son, working for a university development office not far from my home. We get together whenever he visits my city and, when we do, I always bring one thing along, just in case: a deck of cards. We *still* haven't played poker.

I'm glad I didn't try to fix a kid who wasn't even broken. He simply needed his voice heard and acknowledged as valuable.

4

Getting to *A*: Access

Dear Dr. Delisle:

School is ugh. Today in sociology we got into the topic of whether nature or nurture was responsible for development. What better way to teach us this than to give us a worksheet. It gave an opinion on the nature argument and another on the nurture, and then asked us questions about the opinions. It had the same question phrased three different ways. I looked at it and got so pissed. This teaches me nothing. I learn how to copy stuff from the front of a worksheet to the back. High school is basically around to teach us how to take tests. Read a book for English (which I can never bring myself to do), take a test on its content, and then write a paper on whatever meaning the teacher wants us to find in it. School is trying to create the passive, submissive mold of a student that will do whatever teachers want for the sake of a grade.

Ahhhhhhhhhh!

I received this e-mail message from Adam, a young man I had never met but who had read my book *The Gifted Teen Survival Guide* (Galbraith & Delisle, 2011) and thought I might be able to give him some direction in his academic pursuits. When we learned that we lived only about 30 miles apart, we decided to get together and talk—multiple times, it turned out.

You wouldn't suspect it from his message, but Adam was a top scholar and athlete in a prestigious private school, a junior who ranked in the top 10 percent of his class. So, by all appearances, he had played the school game well. But appearances can be deceiving, as inside, Adam was anxious and disappointed. Anxious because he didn't feel this type of education was preparing him for college, and disappointed because most of his teachers weren't astute enough (from Adam's point of view) to notice that the education he was getting lacked rigor and depth.

By most typical measures, Adam would not be considered an underachiever. In the eyes of his teachers, he was anything but. Yet to Adam himself, his sense of disillusionment about what should have been an exceptional education but was, instead, a daily exercise in futility was palpable. I had fears that even in his junior year, he was quickly falling victim to senioritis.

What Adam needed was something that was possible yet hidden to him: *access*. Access to a more relevant curriculum, access to individuals who could help him reach higher academically, and access to his own inner strength to ask for both.

It took a little while to convince Adam that approaching his teachers to ask for something more intellectually sustaining was neither rude nor unreasonable. He started by focusing on one teacher with whom he already had a good rapport—his math teacher—and designed a plan that would prove to her that he knew the content he was supposed to learn. In turn, this teacher excused Adam from lessons that focused on content he had already mastered. Adam proposed that, in place of the usual curriculum, he be allowed to independently research a topic of personal interest (the history of mathematicians across cultures) and present this to the teacher and class in the form of a PowerPoint. At semester's end, Adam had earned an A. He had *truly* earned it and wasn't just given the A for going through the motions in a class that had been barren of new substance.

Adam was not an underachiever, yet the techniques he used to take control of his education are valuable additions to the repertoire of methods educators can use to reach others like him: kids who are intelligent yet underchallenged. In this chapter, I offer several time-tested techniques to advance the education of kids who already know what they are supposed to be learning in class.

Access Strategy 1: Understand and Implement Curriculum Compacting

Imagine the following scenario. You are attending a professional development session and the famed presenter asks the audience to complete a task: write the alphabet, in sequence, and trade papers with another participant to check its accuracy. Suspecting this is some type of nuanced ploy to advance learning in students, you comply. Then the presenter moves on to another topic.

An hour later, this same presenter announces another worthwhile activity: take out a piece of paper and write the alphabet, in sequence, and trade papers with another participant to check its accuracy. Once again, you comply, assuming that there is a method to this apparent madness. After all, you already *know* the alphabet—you proved that an hour ago. However, no discussion follows; you just move on to a new topic.

Returning from lunch break, the presenter introduces *yet another* task: write the alphabet, in sequence, and trade papers with another participant to check its accuracy.

At this point, you would likely do one of three things:

1. Walk out of the session.
2. Ask the presenter, "What's the point of this?"
3. Comply with the request but totally tune out the presenter for the rest of the day as being clueless.

I assume that such a scenario would never occur in a professional development session, yet similar scenarios occur each day in classrooms everywhere. Students are asked, time and again, to complete tasks they have shown multiple times that they have already mastered. From spelling lists to vocabulary words to multiplication tables to memorizing the periodic table, gifted (and other) students are being asked to do something daily that you, as an educator, would not even tolerate for an afternoon: complete academic assignments you have already proven you know how to do.

Enter curriculum compacting. (Disclaimer: I'm not a fan of the term *compacting*, as it brings to mind the thing we compact the most: trash. And since most curricula are not *trash*, I believe the term is a bit harsh.) Curriculum compacting is a concept as old as education, and many teachers past and present would just call it common sense. The term itself was coined by Joseph Renzulli and Linda Smith (1978). In essence, curriculum compacting is the process of assessing student knowledge of basic skills and eliminating or minimizing "practice" of those skills, which opens up time in the school day to explore more advanced or enriching topics. As explained by Heacox (2012), "Likely candidates for compacting are students who already have extensive knowledge of a curriculum topic, have mastered a significant number of skills [the teacher is] planning to present, or are capable of accelerated learning" (p. 142).

My 8th grade teacher invited me to learn by integrating hands-on activities, lectures, humor, music, and my favorite—walks! Once in a while, we'd take 15-minute breaks and walk around campus, simply talking, walking, skipping, or throwing balls. These small breaks gave me a boost for the rest of the day!

Common sense would dictate that the students most likely to be candidates for curriculum compacting are compliant students who, despite their dislike of school, still play by its rules. Indeed, individuals such as Adam should have their curriculum compacted. No argument there. But what about others, such as our selective consumer Marty? He's already not completing basic tasks in class or for homework, and yet we want to reward these belligerent behaviors by eliminating portions of his schoolwork? Short answer: yes. It's not a reward at all to do so but rather an acknowledgment that Marty has mastered what we need him to learn. So, just like you would feel if asked to write the alphabet in sequence for the third time in a day, there is a logical reason for Marty not wanting to continue on this path of non-learning: he's already proven what he's needed to prove. Like you, he'd likely utter, "Let's move on."

In stating this recommendation, I can tell you from experience that curriculum compacting is not a popular option among teachers when it comes to students like Marty. It goes against much of what they learned in their educational psychology and teaching methods courses, and it simply doesn't feel right to bend over backward for someone who has not been willing to complete even the most basic class requirements.

I understand this angst, but I believe it is misplaced. If our ultimate goal is to help even the most recalcitrant students achieve success, then curriculum compacting is even more vital for learners like Marty than it is for students like Adam. For one thing, it says to selective consumers that you know they are skilled in some content areas; this alone is something they may not have heard from many teachers. Second, it puts students and their teachers on the same road—the path to academic success. Third, it gives selective consumers the opportunity to buy in to their own educations; curriculum compacting is not the end point of change but just the beginning.

How so? The basic curriculum is compacted only if the student and teacher come up with alternative assignments or topics of study; just sitting back in class listening to music while other students slog through curriculum you already know is *not* an alternative. If the student is not ready to buy into this agreement, then we return to a curriculum that is both inappropriate and uninteresting to the student.

One concern I hear from middle and high school teachers about curriculum compacting is that it is too difficult to manage with a caseload of 100+ students. This concern would be valid if all of those students needed their curricula compacted—but they won't. The extra up-front time needed to work with the handful of students for whom this is an appropriate and necessary option pays off in the end, as teachers will ultimately spend much less time and angst with high-ability students who are not performing well.

Heacox (2012) gives extensive examples of the mechanics of managing compacting, but all of the suggestions she proposes, though worthwhile, are not as important as one teacher sitting down with one student and sending this message: "I believe you know much of the content of the next few lessons I'm about to teach. How about if I determine if you know as much as I think you do, and if I'm right, I'd like you to propose something else you'd like to learn instead of stuff you already know how to do."

Will this approach always work? Of course not! Some students will say anything to get out of mind-numbing class assignments and then not follow through with what they said they would do instead. Others may not even believe you from the outset, thinking the proposal to be some type of ploy to get them to do work they are fond of shunning. Still others may sincerely want to succeed on these terms but find that their knowledge base or study habits are not as strong as they thought, so they stop trying altogether. Yes, these scenarios could all take place.

By contrast, students may react to curriculum compacting with "For once, a teacher has acknowledged that I know some stuff and, even though I can be a doofus in class, I'm still being given a chance to shine. For the first time in a long time, I'm going to try."

Curriculum compacting may be just the agent of change for students who need *access* to something more than they are getting through their regular classes. If you are able to move beyond the natural reluctance to assist a student who makes your teaching day harder, then you are giving a dose of dignity that students such as this seldom receive.

As you've probably noticed, the curriculum compacting strategy I highlight here is focused more on selective consumers, not under-achievers. As I mentioned in Chapter 1, some strategies will be more appropriate for one type of student than others. Curriculum compacting seems more apt for the Martys in your classroom, not the Sierras. Still, any strategy that works for one student could morph into something similar to help another who, on the surface, appears very different than the one you initially targeted. Therefore, Sierra could also be a candidate for this tried-and-true method of aligning student needs, knowledge, and interests. In fact, it's hard to imagine a scenario where curriculum compacting is *not* a worthwhile approach for those students who know more than they are "supposed to" know at a particular grade level or in a specific subject area.

Access Strategy 2: Design a Set of Remarkable Options

Book reports: boring to write, boring to grade. This timeworn strategy of determining if students read the books they were asked to read and whether they gained any insights from them needs to hit the Refresh button. Too many students (and teachers, I imagine) find the slog through novel after novel lacking . . . novelty.

It's not that the assignment itself is inappropriate; it's that the method of having students document what they've learned gets tedious if, time after time, the format never changes. As we all learned in Differentiation 101 workshops, the educator who truly wants to switch it up has control over the following four elements of classroom interactions, as proposed by Tomlinson (2017):

- The *content* we teach.
- The *processes* we use to present information to students.
- The *products* students complete as evidence of their learning.
- The *physical and emotional learning environments* we create for students.

In this case of access to remarkable options, let's focus on the end product with one powerful example from a 7th grader. Here's the scenario: the entire class had a free choice to read any historical fiction book. The end product they were assigned could take many forms, including:

- Write a letter to the author of the book, focusing on the elements of the novel that the student found interesting, powerful, or confusing.
- Compose either a new last chapter for the book or the first chapter for a sequel.
- Create a mobile that includes various story elements, including plot, theme, characters, and setting.
- Write a song (lyrics and music) that summarizes the plot and theme of the novel.
- Compose a typical book report but without using the letter *e* in the essay.

Dana, a gifted student who enjoyed writing, chose the last option. There was one problem, though: the book she read (*The Red Badge of Courage*) contained a lot of *es* in its title, and the main character's name was Henry, which also included the verboten *e*. Relenting a bit as her teacher, I allowed Dana to use the name of the book and its main character in her book report—but no other exceptions. Here is a portion of Dana's finished product:

The Red Badge of Courage is about a young man's trip from acting in ways of a coward to acting in ways of a strong, audacious army man. A youth, Henry, joins army ranks with aspirations of coming out daring and valiant. Soon though, Henry finds out that actual war contains complications his thoughts did not contain in his original analysis.

 The Red Badge of Courage starts as Henry joins army ranks. Following his signing up, but prior to his first conflagration, fright and worry that valor and stamina might not portray his actions constantly ran through Henry's thoughts.

This book report continues on for another 500 words with nary an *e* in sight. When Dana handed in her completed project, she looked as tired as if she had just run a marathon, which, in a way, she had. It was a marathon of words that gave this always-successful student a run for her intellectual money.

As more evidence of the power of switching up the methods that students use to show mastery, Robert Schultz and I completed an online survey of more than 6,000 gifted children and teens, asking them to share what their teachers had done to make their learning more enticing. Here is just one example (Schultz & Delisle, 2013):

In middle school, I tested out of history and was allowed to do special projects. First, I wrote and directed a film on the French Resistance in WWII, engaging 27 classmates in the production. Also, I did a Civil War project and displayed memorabilia. I had a great teacher who helped me understand that I was valuable, and he kept me soooo busy by having me organize the Special Olympics for my school. When I was in his class, it felt like home.

           —Boy, 16, California (p. 85)

When students are asked to demonstrate their learning in ways that have meaning and purpose, even those who have tuned out previous assignments may begin to oblige. The same curriculum goals can be met through a multiplicity of methods, some designed by teachers and others by students. We all know students who have previously chosen to balk when asked to complete assignments in typical ways but who might be less reluctant when they have access to more options that push the envelope in terms of creativity and innovative learning.

Access Strategy 3:
Take Steps Outside of the Classroom

When you are 13 years old and have a full-page spread devoted to you in *Entrepreneur* magazine, you've got to have done something special. That's exactly the case with Hart Main, a boy from Ohio. Hart's younger sister was participating in a school fundraiser selling candles. Most of the candles were made in what Hart called "girly scents," such as roses and strawberries. Concluding that very few guys would buy those candles, Hart put in $100 of his money and took out a $200 loan from his parents to start a company, Man-Cans, that made candles in soup cans. The aromas that Hart chose were more masculine in nature: freshly cut grass, new baseball mitt, bacon, sawdust, and campfire.

Hart began marketing his candles by bringing them into local stores and asking the owners to take them on consignment. Within a short time, Hart had more than 60 stores, in his hometown of Marysville and across the country, carrying his candles. Most of his initial sales, though, were made through ManCans.com.

That was in 2011. Today, ManCans is still going strong. Hart just began college with a major in economics, which makes sense, considering his venture has now sold more than 300,000 candles. In addition, for each candle sold, Hart donates a meal to one of 25 homeless shelters located in four different states. That's more than 300,000 donated meals to date!

Hart's scent menu has also expanded, and you can now purchase ManCans that smell like Memphis BBQ, gunpowder, flapjacks, and more. In case you'd like to follow his lead, Hart and his dad coauthored a book, *One Candle, One Meal* (Main & Main, 2015), which describes both his project's history and the reasons behind his philanthropic efforts.

A year into his project, Hart mentioned that he would continue spearheading his business, despite needing to concentrate on school. Here's my question: Why couldn't ManCans have *become* his "school"? When you consider the many skills it takes to create, market, and operate a successful venture like ManCans (e.g., math, reading, chemistry, communications), making this project a part of his curriculum would have been an ideal way to link his learning to the real world of business.

Now think of the underachievers or selective consumers with whom you have worked or lived. How might they react if something of note they were pursuing outside of school became a central focus of the work they completed *inside* of school? This vital yet often ignored linkage is one more option to consider when it comes to helping highly able students who perform poorly gain access to their own possibilities.

> My math mentor got me excited about learning by not necessarily teaching what was part of the curriculum but teaching me little "side topics" that she thought I might find interesting. When teachers teach us things they don't "have to" teach, I get more excited about and engaged in learning.

Luckily, we don't have to wait for our students to become entrepreneurs before we invite them to bring their worlds into our schools, as many so-called extracurricular options are there for the taking. National History Day is a case in point. Founded in 1974, this nonprofit education organization offers year-long academic programs involving students in grades 6–12. Every year begins with a theme (e.g., the 2017 theme was Taking a Stand in History), and students create original research on that theme after they have narrowed their topic to a manageable size. Annually, more than 500,000 students around the world compete in National History Day, with a culminating summit held each June in Washington, D.C.

The theme offered at the first competition in 1980 was The Individual in History, which is a focus that has been repeated three times over the years—most recently in 2009. It was then that two 8th graders from Idaho—Marissa Lords and Tyler Stephens—took this theme and decided to find Buster Hill. Buster Hill was a boy from Connecticut who, during World War II, pledged to purchase war bonds and stamps until the war ended. Indeed, he was an individual in history. Through some research, Lords and Stephens learned that in the 1940s, the government sent blank scrapbooks to schools across the country to document students' pledges. Searching eBay, these two young researchers found and purchased one of these long-ago scrapbooks, replete with kids' names, including Buster Hill's.

Using every Internet search tool at their disposal, Marissa and Tyler found and contacted every child whose name was in the scrapbook from Hazardville Elementary School, hoping that at least one would respond. Many did, including Alice Moody Webb, who recalled the project and offered her help in finding Buster (she was so impressed that current-day students were interested in what happened so long ago). By the time their year-long research was completed, Lords and Stephens had compiled a 32-page bibliography of the primary sources they had located, including interviews with many of the people whose names were in the scrapbook. But Buster Hill? He was never found.

Still, this 8th grade dynamic duo went on to win first place in the Idaho National History Day competition and, when they went to the national event, they were asked to present their research at the

Smithsonian's National Museum of American History. A few days later, they won first place, even though they never did find their man, Buster Hill.

Prior to the national competition, in an interview with *River City Weekly*—his hometown newspaper—Tyler questioned why it was that many adults think that only they have the power to make a difference in the world. Their project, and the efforts of kids such as Buster Hill, proved otherwise. An individual in history—from Idaho, Connecticut, or somewhere else—just might be a kid.

Why does National History Day work? Here's a hint:

Students become writers, filmmakers, web designers, playwrights, and artists as they create unique contemporary expressions of history. . . . National History Day not only transports classrooms back in time during the school year, it transforms young minds forever. (National History Day, 2016, para. 1–2)

Virtually every content area covered in school has some type of option or competition similar in focus to National History Day. These kinds of events engage students in high-level research or elaborative discovery. The Johns Hopkins Center for Talented Youth (2017) is a fantastic repository for hundreds of such contests, including these:

- **Quill and Scroll Society International Photo Contest** (www.quillandscroll.org): This high school competition provides awards in writing, photography, multimedia, blogging, and yearbook design.
- **Scholastic Art and Writing Awards** (www.artandwriting. org): Among the largest competitions of its type, more than 320,000 7th through 12th graders participated in 2016. More than 2,500 winning students and their educators were honored in a ceremony at Carnegie Hall.

- **Google Science Fair** (www.googlesciencefair.com/en): Open to students age 13–18, this international, online competition gives awards in multiple categories and is cosponsored by groups such as National Geographic, Virgin Galactic, and *Scientific American.*
- **MathCounts** (www.mathcounts.org): Founded in 1983, this live, in-person competition open to students in grades 6–8 holds regional and national events. Schools compete in teams, and preparation is offered through a free resource, which contains more than 250 creative problems that meet the national standards set by the National Council of Teachers of Mathematics.

Often, a school's stellar scholars are the ones who are invited or encouraged to participate in these intensive events—as they should be. However, students whose intellects are high but whose typical academic performance is low can be equally impressive participants in these extracurricular options. Denying access to these learning opportunities until students perform "up to par" (as is sometimes the case) is a policy based on punishment, not possibility. True academic turnaround for some students may occur in competitions such as these, where real-world impact is one of the primary motivators.

Access Strategy 4: Pay Attention to the Pace of Classroom Instruction

In Detroit, I met a polite and academically successful high school junior named Lydia who had a checkered past: she had been suspended in kindergarten! It seems that, while in kindergarten, Lydia's teacher would distribute basic worksheets, such as copying letters and matching colors—skills that Lydia had mastered well before the school year began. Therefore, she would work through her assignments quickly and accurately and then sit quietly until her classmates had finished their work.

This daily waiting quickly grew tiresome, so Lydia opted for something different. She would move from desk to desk, completing the worksheets for her classmates so they could all move on to something else that was more fun. Every day, her teacher tried to stop her, but Lydia was fast. Catching her in the act was like playing a game of whack-a-mole. Parent conferences ensued, but changes in Lydia's behavior were negligible, and she was deemed too immature for kindergarten. As a result, she was temporarily suspended from school.

> I think that one thing that really helps me is when we take days in class to just do individual work quietly. This allows for students to do work their own way and for the teachers to see how their students actually work.

Obviously, she eventually reenrolled and, in subsequent years, found ways to entertain herself when the waiting game grew tedious. She'd read a book, write a poem, or daydream of a school where she could simply move through curriculum at a pace that matched her intellect. But why did she need to wait when there was so much of the world to explore?

The issue of pacing is one that complements another strategy cited earlier: curriculum compacting. In this case, though, it is not the content of the curriculum that is the focus but rather the speed with which students can move through it. For students who do poorly on purpose, setting the pace is yet another strategy that gives them access to learning.

Heacox and Cash (2014) offer some specific strategies for accelerating the pace of instruction for students who need and benefit from such modifications. Here are some of their ideas (p. 18):

- Create the course syllabus with clear objectives, including what students will know, understand, and be able to do after each lesson, so that they know what to expect.
- Implement some strategies for a flipped classroom, wherein students do reading and preparation at home, leaving most

classroom time for investigating new ideas and clarifying any confusion about the reading assignments.

- Have all of the resources for the teaching unit readily available ahead of time and make them accessible to students. Encourage them to add, delete, or replace portions of the unit that they can prove they already know.
- During lessons, offer one or two examples or models and then move forward. Spend most classroom time investigating and wrestling with controversial issues, complex problems, and in-depth conversation.
- Use brief warm-up activities at the beginning of each class that engage students immediately and set the stage for the lesson. These "hooks" can be brainteasers, questions about controversial issues, logic problems, or random thoughts or quotes to explore.

For this latter point—using hooks to engage students—one of my favorite resources is The Big Question, which appears in every issue of *The Atlantic* magazine. Recent questions included the following:

- Who was the worst leader of all time?
- Who is the most interesting family in history?
- What concept most needs a word in the English language?
- What fictional school would you most like to attend?
- What accident most changed the course of history?
- What is the most significant fad of all time?
- Who is the most influential teenager of all time?
- What is the greatest scam in history?

Each question is answered by people of many persuasions: artists, politicians, actors, economists, magicians, authors, journalists, professors, and more. (You can access these intriguing questions and answers at www.theatlantic.com/magazine/category/big-question.) I've yet to have a teenager, achieving or otherwise, who isn't fascinated by the variety of responses given to these intriguing queries.

Setting the pace of instruction to match students' minds can definitely be a juggling act for teachers, but for the few students whose performance is pegged to the need to proceed through curriculum at an accelerated speed, it is one more strategy that gives them access to the knowledge they crave.

Access Strategy 5:
Introduce Time Management and Study Skills to Students

No matter who you are or where you live, we all share a common reality: each day has only 24 hours in it. Some of us (and our students) are expert jugglers with these daily 1,440 minutes, managing to complete tasks on our to-do lists with ease and clarity. Others are somewhat (or terribly) challenged when it comes to completing what needs to be finished, operating as if deadlines were more like suggestions than mandates.

For students who underachieve academically, time management is often a major hurdle to overcome. Given several tasks to complete—homework in four subjects, household chores and other family responsibilities, job or college applications to fill out—some underachieving students will choose the path of least resistance. They'll do nothing at all. Friends, social media, games, and other distractions will occupy their time, yet the blowback received from parents and teachers about "being lazy" or "unmotivated" continue to dog capable students who just can't get their managerial acts together.

More books and websites than I can count have been written about how to manage time, and many of them offer good guidance and practical strategies. It's not my intent to detail here a topic as large as time management or to replicate the age-old suggestions of writing down your daily goals, keeping checklists you can cross off, or getting advice from people who manage time well. When it comes to underachievers, one of the most basic reasons for failing to use time well is more an internally based belief than any type of external strategy.

> These internal beliefs or values are what give you the power to do what needs to be done. Remember that what works for someone else might not work for you, keep trying various techniques you read about or hear about, and stay focused on your values until you find one or more methods that are a good fit for your learning style, personality, energy level, intellect, and needs. (Galbraith & Delisle, 2011, p. 105)

As previously mentioned, some students who underachieve would rather get a low grade, or no grade at all, than risk "defeat" by earning a *B* and being told they could do better. Psychologically, it makes sense to put off doing something that you believe you'll be criticized for anyway, as it is difficult for adults to critique work that never gets completed.

Time management is not a magic elixir that will turn every student who underachieves into an academic superstar. Still, it is a helpful tool to share, and, in fact, some of the best people to help with time management issues are other classmates who have mastered the art of multitasking. Sometimes, the same advice or suggestions given by someone your own age instead of an adult authority figure makes a positive difference.

The same goes for a related topic—developing study habits. For many intelligent students who underachieve, there is a good reason their study habits are limited. They've never needed to have any. In elementary school, many of these students earned high grades without ever lifting an intellectual finger, so while classmates were learning the benefits of note taking, organizing, and setting aside time to review before tests, these students who now underachieve simply showed up, took the exam, and earned an *A*. Simple as that.

It is very helpful when teachers congratulate you when you succeed instead of scolding you when you don't. A few of my middle school teachers followed this policy, and it helped me and a lot of my friends succeed.

Eventually, though, that stopped working. Although classmates who learned how to study continued to reap the benefits of those good study habits, the once successful students who seldom if ever opened a book before a test are now left in the dust. They have no reservoir of study methods to fall back on, so they either stop trying altogether or they use study methods (like cramming) that don't work often or well.

However, there are specific study strategies that actually do work, whether you are in middle or graduate school. Professor Robert A. Bjork (n.d.), codirector of UCLA's Learning and Forgetting Lab (yes, it's actually called that) has identified seven interrelated study techniques, including these:

- **Allocate attention efficiently:** Bjork believes that if people divide their attention between two tasks, both tasks suffer. Therefore, taking one task at a time, students can figure out ways to tackle the stuff they're supposed to learn. If they're fond of highlighting texts with yellow markers, they need to know that this is a passive activity that doesn't help retain information. If a book's pages are covered with more yellow than not, the highlighter should be put aside and replaced with a pen or pencil. Students should then write the crux of particular paragraphs in the margins, which is an active process that engages the mind, helps with retention, and serves as a guide to the book's most salient points.
- **Vary your studying techniques:** It is often mentioned that students should have one place at home and at school for the express purpose of studying. Bjork disagrees. He has found that students actually retain more information

if they alternate settings in which they study. If students have trouble understanding a concept, they should review it several times in the different settings they've selected. Also, they shouldn't even try studying for hours on end without a break; a study break of at least five minutes per hour—more for younger students—is essential. This is especially good advice if students find that they've just read several pages of text and have no idea what they just read.

- **Space your study over time:** Bjork's prescription is to study one subject, take a break, go to subject two, take a break, go back and revisit the first subject, take another break, return to the second subject, and take another break . . . until tomorrow. Repeat as needed.

- **Organize and structure yourself:** If students have to read a long book chapter, they often begin on the first page and just move on through to its conclusion. According to Bjork's research, this is not the best approach. Instead, students should begin by reading the chapter summary or conclusion, followed by a review of the chapter's subheadings, which are almost always an advance guide on its most salient topics. While reading, they should take notes on the most important points, so when they return to the chapter later, they can begin by reviewing their own notes.

These and other of Bjork's methods are common-sense suggestions backed up by cognitive psychology—a fine combination. In addition to Bjork's ideas, you might also suggest that your students vary *how* they take in information. Visual learners may prefer charts and graphs over printed texts, whereas auditory learners might find recorded lectures more appealing. Writers might opt to compose a summary of what they just read, highlighting the main points they want to recall later. Each of us has particular learning preferences; we should urge our students to explore their own. Just remember—as with basketball shoes and bikinis, there is no such thing as one-size-fits-all.

With kids who underachieve, telling them to study harder or work smarter is banal advice that is too vague to be useful. Not all of Bjork's strategies will work for everyone, yet when a student starts with an empty bag of tricks regarding study strategies, the specific ideas highlighted here can offer both guidance and direction.

Summary

I've never met a student who wakes up in the morning with the hope of looking dumb in front of classmates. I've also rarely met a teacher who enters the classroom with the goal of discovering a student's inner flaws or inadequacies and putting them on display for others to see. With smart students who underachieve, though, there are times when the dual frustration felt by both student and teacher set up conditions that are less than conducive to learning. Sometimes, our students don't try because they are asked to do work they believe is beneath their intellectual level; other times, teachers feel compelled to have even the most capable students complete basic work so that a grade can be recorded.

In classroom situations where there is a tug of war between what a student and a teacher see as a beneficial learning activity, the short-term victor is usually the person in charge: the teacher. He or she controls what access to give to advanced learning opportunities, which assignments to shorten or eliminate altogether, and what options exist for having students "show what they know" in ways that are either innovative or stultifyingly dull.

The student, too, has some control, for it is up to him or her to decide whether to comply with teacher requests. Yet when a conflict arises between what students and teachers see as valuable, it is not uncommon for the underachieving student to shut down altogether, resulting in even more conflict and disappointment on everyone's part.

At times like these, both student and teacher need to take a breath, count to 10, and rewind the tape that has produced this educational cacophony. Once reset, dialogue can begin again, often initiated by a teacher brave enough to say, "Look, we've hit a rough patch, you and I, when it comes to my assignments and expectations. Can we talk?"

Giving *access* to students who underachieve begins with just such a dialogue. It says to the student that we are willing to listen, not just impose our ideas without regard to his or her needs. It also implies that we are willing to open doors so that our students might more readily take control of their learning. In communicating the skills highlighted in this chapter, you are inviting students to walk through that door of learning with you.

In the Maori culture, there is a saying: *Naku te rourou nau te rourou ka ora ai te iwi.* When translated, this means, "With your basket and my basket, the people will live." This principle can apply not just in New Zealand but in classrooms everywhere when teachers and students together contribute to each other's "basket" in support of mutual learning and respect.

5

Getting to *A*: Advocacy

D'Andre was a former middle school student of mine who was smarter than his grades indicated. He spent a lot of time in the principal's office for various infractions, causing him to be perceived by peers as not only a dumb kid but also a bad one. D'Andre wrote about his classmates' perceptions of him:

> They never understood that my frustrations were due to my inability to believe in myself, which made me a lonely child. When I realized that people thought I was dumb, bad, and incapable, I was infuriated that I had picked these labels for myself. I could no longer blame my image on poverty, on teachers, or on other students; I had created it. This revelation led to the decision that changed the course of my life—the decision to run for class president. (Galbraith & Delisle, 2011, p. 240)

D'Andre's story is one of personal redemption. He was elected to be his 8th grade class president, and he subsequently became a role model and leader for others. For the first time in his life, he achieved top grades. *Also* for the first time in his life, D'Andre realized that the person most in charge of his education was . . . D'Andre. His upward trajectory continued. He graduated high school as an honors student, captain of his track team, and class president for all four years. While in high school, D'Andre helped raise more than $5,000 for victims of a natural disaster and formed a club to help underachieving African American males. College brought him to the Ivy League, where he graduated in 2015. In reflecting on the personal progress he made, D'Andre wrote, "Although our individual struggles are what make us uniquely great, those struggles can also hinder us from tapping into that greatness. From my perspective, life is just a series of chances, and those who succeed are the ones who are prepared and audacious enough to seize them (Galbraith & Delisle, 2011, p. 241).

Although D'Andre attributes much of his success to the adults who began to believe in him during 8th grade, there is no discounting the importance of D'Andre becoming his own best advocate. Running headlong into the winds of low expectations, D'Andre turned himself around by realizing the power of his own intentions.

Advocacy Strategy 1: Help Our Students Become Their Own Best Advocates

Self-advocacy is an offshoot of the Civil Rights Movement of the 1960s, where people of color were taking charge of their lives by demanding liberties that had been long overdue. Most recently, groups such as SABE (Self Advocates Becoming Empowered) have played a similar role in ensuring that individuals with developmental disabilities have a stake in life decisions—without undue influence or control by others—that affect them personally. Health care rights, educational access rights, and housing rights are just a few of the focus areas for self-advocates with this population.

Until recently, though, there have been few resources for students to become their own advocates to achieve an appropriate education. Deb Douglas, a long-time coordinator of gifted programs, put together an impressive set of ideas for students—those who underachieve and those who succeed but are still dissatisfied with the education they receive—to take charge of their own learning. Her definition of *self-advocacy* is one based on positive change and mutual respect: "Self-advocacy is the process of recognizing and meeting the needs specific to one's learning ability without compromising the dignity of oneself or others" (Douglas, n.d., para 1).

> I do have friends who are smart but don't care about school;
> I have been this way myself. It is easier to learn when teachers
> don't shove information down your throat but instead work
> with you to help you learn what you need to know.

Why is self-advocacy important for students who underachieve? For many of them, school is a daily dose of ennui, and they believe that teachers are the culprits in maintaining a system that doesn't fit their needs. It's a blame game and, whether expressed silently or vocally, students who underachieve accuse their teachers of boring them on purpose. Too frequently, these students tune out (or drop out) because they don't believe they have any control over their educational lives. In essence, school is something done *to* them, not *with* them.

Douglas's ideas about self-advocacy change all that. She focuses on the following four principles and shares them with middle and high school students, inviting them to become active participants in meaningful educational change (Douglas, 2018).

Step 1: Understand your rights and responsibilities. Each student has a right to a rigorous and meaningful education and, therefore, is responsible for taking an active role in making this happen.

Step 2: Assess and reflect on your learner profile: abilities and interests, strengths and weaknesses, learning styles and habits. *How* you learn is as important as *what* you learn, but before students can expect changes in instructional methods or content, they must take a personal inventory of their learning strengths and gaps, as well as itemize their own interests and learning preferences.

Step 3: Match your attributes to options and opportunities. The more specific students can be about what they already know, how they can prove it to a teacher's satisfaction, and what they would like to do specifically instead of the content they've already mastered, the more likely educators will be willing to cooperate.

Step 4: Connect with advocates who can support your goals. Although self-advocacy efforts begin with individual students, there is no need to have them travel this road alone. Which adults in their lives might be able to support their efforts with advice and emotional back-up?

Not every attempt to self-advocate will be successful. Some teachers are more willing to listen than others, and if the relationship between student and teacher is already strained due to previous student noncompliance, the issue of trust might be a major barrier to overcome. What's my advice to students in this regard? Begin with a teacher who is both approachable and malleable rather than one who is distant and dogmatic. In addition, as previously stated, the more specific the alternative educational options are that the student raises with the teacher, the more likely success will be achieved.

It's also important to remember that when a smart student is not doing well in class, frustration is shared by both the learner and the teacher. Developing and implementing a specific self-advocacy plan may be a way to chart a path where success for all is possible.

Advocacy Strategy 2:
Introduce Students to the Ten Tips
for Talking to Teachers

Think back to your own time in middle and high school. If you're like me, there was a solid line of demarcation between students and teachers. In other words, teachers distributed knowledge and content, and students were expected to absorb it. In most schools, as the grade levels got higher so did the separation of students by either perceived ability or academic achievement. By the time junior year of high school rolled around, most students were in their core classes with the same batch of students, irrespective of the subject matter. The incorrect assumption of "smart in one thing, smart in everything" was definitely at play.

This scenario still exists in the majority of today's high schools, so it makes sense that in these classrooms where intellectual or academic ability is within a relatively narrow range, most students find something new and relevant to learn. That's not always the case, of course, and when it isn't, what is a student to do? I don't recall being taught how to talk with a teacher so my curriculum was a better match with my abilities or interests so I often just sat there, paying attention when something the teacher said caught my attention but mostly sitting back and daydreaming about being anyplace other than my Algebra II classroom. My guess is that most of you did the same; you simply went through the academic motions, earned a good grade, and learned very little in the subjects in which you were already adept.

It doesn't have to be this way. Given the proper tools and guidance, even students who underachieve can learn how to approach a teacher in a respectful and professional way in order to find a better match between what is offered in class and what their abilities and classroom performance indicate they already know. Consider, then, the ten tips for talking to teachers (Figure 5.1). Developed over 25 years ago, this set of suggestions has helped thousands of students make substantial improvements to their daily school lives. This list provides realistic and respectful strategies students can use to approach almost any teacher if they want to have an honest discussion about the benefits of an education that is matched to their individual interests and competencies.

As Figure 5.1 indicates, the first thing students must do before having such a discussion is act as professionals do when they want to review an issue of importance—schedule a meeting. Change seldom happens if a student happens to catch a teacher in the hall between classes and asks for something different, but if both student and teacher schedule a dedicated time to talk, then that is the first step in potentially positive change. Ahead of time, the student must prepare an agenda, perhaps by making a list of requests he or she can refer to during the meeting (Tip #3). If the student doesn't choose his or her words carefully (Tip #4), then the meeting could sink faster than the *Titanic* (i.e., saying "book reports suck" is unlikely to gain much traction with teachers). The remainder of the 10 tips focus on how a suggested change would benefit the student, academically or otherwise. There are a few other caveats for the student to recognize; for example, the teacher may be overburdened with too many other students or responsibilities to act on this request immediately. However, if the student feels like the teacher is simply saying no without a legitimate reason, or if an air of disrespect permeates the meeting, then it might be time to engage a guidance counselor or another teacher. This is not to be used as a threat by the student—that never works—but if the student has approached the teacher with respect and a good set of listening ears, then taking the next step is warranted.

I can hear the critics now. Why would a teacher want to bend over backward for a kid who has been reluctant to do the same in return? My answer is simple. If nothing else has worked up to this point—punishment, loss of privileges, parent conferences—then

Figure 5.1

Ten Tips for Talking to Teachers

Are you having a problem with a class or an assignment? Can you see room for improvement in how a subject is taught? Do you have a better idea for a special project or term paper? Don't just tell your friends. Talk to the teacher!

Many students have told us that they don't know how to go about doing this. The following suggestions are meant to make it easier for everyone—students and teachers.

1. Make an appointment to meet and talk. This shows the teacher that you're serious and you have some understanding of his or her busy schedule. Tell the teacher about how much time you'll need, be flexible, and don't be late.

2. If you know other students who feel the way you do, consider approaching the teacher together. There's strength in numbers. If a teacher hears the same thing from four or five people, he or she is more likely to do something about it.

3. Think through what you want to say before you go into your meeting with the teacher. Write down your questions or concerns. Make a list of the items you want to cover. You may even want to copy your list for the teacher so both of you can consult it during your meeting. (Or consider giving it to the teacher ahead of time.)

4. Choose your words carefully. Example: Instead of saying, "I hate doing reports; they're boring and a waste of time," try, "Is there some other way I could satisfy this requirement? Could I do a video instead?" Strike the word "boring" from your vocabulary. It's a buzzword for teachers.

5. Don't expect the teacher to do all of the work or propose all of the answers. Be prepared to make suggestions, offer solutions, even recommend resources. The teacher will appreciate that you took the initiative.

6. Be diplomatic, tactful, and respectful. Teachers have feelings, too. And they're more likely to be responsive if you remember that the purpose of your meeting is conversation, not confrontation.

7. Focus on what you need, not on what you think the teacher is doing wrong. The more the teacher learns about you, the more he or she will be able to help. The more defensive the teacher feels, the less he or she will want to help.

(continued)

Figure 5.1 (*continued*)

---

8. Don't forget to listen. Strange but true, many students need practice in this essential skill. The purpose of your meeting isn't just to hear yourself talk.

9. Bring your sense of humor. Not necessarily the joke-telling sense of humor, but the one that lets you laugh at yourself and your own misunderstandings and mistakes.

10. If your meeting isn't successful, get help from another adult. "Successful" doesn't necessarily mean that you emerged victorious. Even if the teacher denies your request, your meeting can still be judged successful. If you had a real conversation—if you communicated openly, listened carefully, and respected each other's point of view—then congratulate yourself on a great meeting. If the air crackled with tension, the meeting fell apart, and you felt disrespected (or acted disrespectful), then it's time to bring in another adult. Suggestions: a guidance counselor, the gifted program coordinator, or another teacher you know and trust who seems likely to support you and advocate for you. Once you've found help, approach your teacher and try again.

Source: From *When Gifted Kids Don't Have All the Answers* (pp. 153–154), by J. Galbraith and J. Delisle, 2015, Minneapolis, MN: Free Spirit Publishing. Reprinted with permission.

we must, as professional educators, keep an eye on the ultimate student prize: possible success. The worst that could happen would be that the student doesn't keep his or her end of the bargain and simply slacks off in new or different ways. If that occurs, then the teacher has every right to call out the student's lack of follow-through and return to the prescribed curriculum that the student claimed wasn't a good fit. However, if the student has gone through this "Ten Tips" process with energy and honesty, the chances of failing to live up to these new expectations are lessened. For students who might be trying this self-advocacy strategy for the first time, it is a good idea to role-play with another adult before approaching the teacher in question. A trial run through the various steps might raise some pitfalls to avoid and some techniques or statements that seem particularly effective.

> Some teachers believe that just because we are "smart kids" that we
> should do 10 times the work or be doubly mature due to our intellects.
> Sometimes, they need to remember that we are just teenagers.

No matter how intelligent the student, there may be times when he or she needs to be reminded of the obligations and commitments of their negotiated plan. Nevertheless, if you, as a teacher, have been willing to take this leap of faith with some of your students, then you've already opened the door for honest communication. Generally, students who can achieve but choose not to don't work for a grade; they work for a person. By listening and responding positively to students who advocate for an education more in sync with their individual needs, you are showing unbridled respect for those who may not feel they have received much of it in the past.

One final caveat. If there is a student in your class whom you believe can benefit from doing something different than what is generally offered, share the Ten Tips with him or her and offer an invitation: "Hey, Layla, I know from watching you that you already know much of the curriculum I'm about to teach. You might want to take a look at this and see if there's something you want to do instead of what I'm teaching the other students. Just a thought."

Whether your invitation is accepted or not, you've sent the message that both teacher and student might be on the same page when it comes to learning.

Advocacy Strategy 3: Try to Pull the Plug on Perfectionism

The two advocacy strategies suggested so far work quite well with selective consumers (i.e., the Martys in our classrooms). With those students whose underachievement is based on a true lack of belief in their own abilities (i.e., the Sierras you teach), though, they might not be as appropriate. Remember, underachievers like Sierra truly value what a teacher offers in terms of curriculum, so it is unlikely that they see the benefit of advocating for something different.

However, that is not the case with perfectionism. Although selective consumers rarely are afflicted with perfectionism, under-achievers suffer from it chronically (Van Gemert, 2017). In one respect, this is ironic, because if underachievers' confidence and performance are already low, worrying about being perfect seems like an anomaly. Still, it is present more often than not, resulting in work that is apologized for while it is being handed to the teacher. Familiar comments include "I know this is really bad work. I'm sorry I couldn't do better." Alternatively, assignments are turned in with so many erasures that the paper itself resembles confetti, or work isn't turned in at all because it was "forgotten" at home. And when it comes time for a test, many perfectionistic underachievers go into full panic mode, paralyzed at the thought of not knowing something they are supposed to have learned.

Each of these occurrences is a sign that perfectionism is the culprit working against students' success. As Whitmore (1980) said about perfectionism in her study of young underachievers, "This personality characteristic . . . is the most overlooked and influen-tial of those traits distinctly associated with individuals of superior intelligence. . . . This motivating force seems to be a desire to prove to the world that they are adequate and worthy" (pp. 145–146). If this is true for even successful students with high abilities, imagine the effect it can have on students who underachieve and feel defeated with nearly every academic task.

There are several ways to address this topic with students, but the first step is for an adult who knows the underachieving student well enough to have a private conversation (perhaps more than one) that addresses some of the specific fears underlying this perfection-istic behavior. Questions can include the following examples:

- How do you feel when you do something successfully?
- Do you have difficulty enjoying what you are doing now because you keep thinking about what you have to do later?
- Do you ever think to yourself, "If I can't do something perfectly, what's the point in trying at all?"
- How do you think people will react if you're less than perfect?

After these questions (whose answers might be accompanied by tears), try this next set:

- Can you recall a time you succeeded when you didn't think you would?
- Do you ever get involved in anything where nobody wins and nobody loses—where you just have fun? Do you enjoy these times?
- When you look around at the adults in your life, are any of them perfect or do they sometimes make mistakes?
- If I told you I was going to give you *A*s in all of your subjects so you could just go ahead and learn stuff, what would you think about that?

Perfectionism doesn't go away on its own, and not talking about it candidly with the afflicted student leaves an open emotional wound that only festers over time. However, once the groundwork has been laid and you have discussed the issue, small steps can be taken to put perfectionism into perspective. Using real-world examples and a dose of humor, positive changes might just begin to occur.

Show students how mistakes can sometimes turn into great accomplishments. Begin by asking your students what the following items have in common: cheese, chocolate chip cookies, penicillin, sticky notes, and Silly Putty. What is the link they all share? Each was invented by accident. Likewise, what is similar about the work of Charles Darwin, Linus Pauling, Fred Hoyle, and Albert Einstein? Even though they were all responsible for groundbreaking scientific work, each was also responsible for making some brilliant mistakes.

Books such as *Mistakes That Worked* (Jones, 1991) and *Brilliant Blunders* (Livio, 2013) show how many everyday inventions were created by accident and reveal the benefits of making mistakes.

Personalize "failures" by talking about some of your own. For example, I have written many books, but three have been rejected more than 50 times—and I have the letters to prove it! Sharing these rejection letters with my students is always a humbling and humorous experience. (I also remind them that I get royalty checks for the books that weren't rejected!) A second example is the one I mentioned in Chapter 1 about my Aunt Peggy who, when I received a PhD at the age of 28, reminded me that "I could've been a *real* doctor—the kind of doctor who helps people." Until the day she died, Aunt Peggy saw me as an underachiever because I didn't become a medical doctor. Personal stories such as these can be the catalyst for great conversations with students about how some people are willing to judge your life without asking permission to do so. With relevant, personal examples, the seed is planted so students can be successful by their own standards, not someone else's.

Give your students verbal ammunition to let others know how their expectations affect them. For instance,

- With parents: "I know you like it when I get *As*, and I always try to do so, but I'm in AP Chemistry instead of the standard course, and it's tougher than I thought it would be. Do I have your support even if my grades aren't the highest?"
- With teachers: "When you call on me in class and say, 'Well, there's at least one student I can rely on to get the right answer,' I feel both pressured and embarrassed, even if you mean it as a compliment."
- With friends: "Even though I'm in the gifted classes and you aren't, that doesn't mean I get everything right. Just like you, I'm not a genius."

Allow students to explore their inner psyches. Sometimes, underachieving students need help putting their lives into perspective. The reassuring words of others, such as this example, can help:

Our deepest fear is not that we are inadequate. Our deepest fear is that we are powerful beyond measure. It is our light, not our darkness that most frightens us. We ask ourselves, "Who am I to be brilliant, gorgeous, talented, fabulous?" Actually, who are you *not* to be? . . . Your playing small does not serve the world. There is nothing enlightened about shrinking so that other people won't feel insecure around you. We are all meant to shine. (Williamson, 1992, pp. 190–191)

Williamson's words are dramatic—perhaps too dramatic for some young people. If this is the case for your students, offer something else that might hit a little closer to home, such as the essay in Figure 5.2. This essay, written by a perfectionistic, high-achieving teenager, puts the issue in focus in a powerful, personal way.

Watch your words and the unintentional effects they might have. When an adult says something like "You did a great job on this assignment, *but* . . .," the only thing a perfectionistic student is likely to remember is what comes after the word *but*. Human nature being what it is, when most people receive a compliment simultaneously with an urge to improve, they focus on what they haven't done well rather than what was accomplished. This is especially noticeable with those who underachieve. In fact, even if a teacher compliments a student without mentioning a need to improve, the most perfectionistic of these underachieving students will still add their own caveat, such as, "Well, I would have done a better job if I had another week to work on it." If students come back with their own urge to improve, stop them in mid-sentence, reminding them that the work they did was of high quality. If it is the case that the student needs to improve in some areas, it's fine to bring that up—later. Remember, coupling a compliment with an urge to do better is a "kick in the *but*" that perfectionistic students can live without.

Figure 5.2

Off-center and Smudged by Amanda Rose Martin

Of all the things I've ever done, I've never been terrible at any of them. The few things that managed to go over my head were polished off with a bit of extra study and work . . . surprisingly enough, the first class that I was terrible at was photography; that was where I realized for the first time that I wasn't perfect. And I panicked.

An elective taken in your senior year (of high school) shouldn't be your hardest class, but for me it was. Walking into the darkroom for the first time was overwhelming. I made my way over to an enlarger and prodded it until another girl took pity on me and helped me locate the button that turned the light on. That day, I ruined about 10 sheets of photo paper—not a cheap thing to waste.

Somehow, one photograph managed to turn out right. It was a waterfall scene I had taken the week before. The picture was sharp and in focus. Elated, I completed the development process and showed the finished product to my teacher.

"Now *that's* a job well done!" he said.

When my teacher smiled at me and handed me back my photograph, I realized something. Not many things in my life had meant as much to me as that picture *because I had to work for it*. For the first time in my life, I had been clueless and confused . . . and for the first time in my life, something else happened.

As I admired my photograph, I realized that its borders weren't even. There were white dust specks that had made their home on my lovingly developed negative. Yet, I realized that in spite of all this imperfection, I cherished my photo.

Those first few weeks of photography class were extremely difficult for me, but in the end, I discovered something that would be more important to me than my grade. Before this experience, I felt everything I did had to be perfect; in fact, *being* perfect was a necessity to me, as essential to life as breathing. I found, though, that I was wrong with this assumption. I found that *imperfection* gives something character, a personality, and a story. The defects in my photograph added to, not subtracted from, my accomplishment.

My photograph (it now has a place on the wall above my bed) is in focus and its subject is sharp. Yes, it may be a bit off-center. Sure, there may be a few dust spots on it. But after all that, this photograph is still something to show the world.

I am that photograph, off-center and smudged, but all-the-better for it.

Source: From *The Gifted Teen Survival Guide* (pp. 89–90), by J. Galbraith and J. Delisle, 2011, Minneapolis, MN: Free Spirit Publishing. Adapted with permission.

When a smart student is underachieving and making excuses for not completing work, teachers should never enforce the idea that the student just needs to "start doing their work." While laziness is never good, if the teacher knows that a particular student could do exponentially better, a few special instructions as to how to do so could be very helpful. Also, positivity can make all the difference in a student's success.

Often, perfectionistic students are leery of pursuing something new; they fear they won't be successful, or they'd rather stick with the tried-and-true than risk doing something original. Adults try to help (but don't) by saying something like "I don't care about your grade as long as you try your best." Perfectionistic students will only remember the words *your best*. Of course, the intended message had nothing to do with performing perfectly; it was meant as encouragement to explore something different. The solution to this one is easy. Simply say, "I don't care about your grade as long as you try." *That's* what you meant, but taking the onus of peak performance off the table and asking only that a student *try* may send a comforting message to someone afraid of failing to reach preconceived expectations.

Another statement you should try to avoid is one that underachieving, perfectionistic students hear all too often: "You're not working up to your potential." Such a message, often delivered at parent-teacher conferences, is wrong on many levels. First, it implies that you (the adult) *know* the extent of this student's abilities, but you're not going to get specific about how high they are. Second, it is such a vague statement that no student could possibly know how to interpret it. You've given no indicators as to when the student will have performed adequately. Third, instead of focusing on what the student *has* accomplished, this statement beams in on whatever it is that has *not* been done, the specifics of which are often left unstated.

A better approach for a student with high abilities that have not yet been attained is to talk about actual work that *has* been completed, asking the student's own opinion of what was done well, what could have been done better, and what steps (if any) can be taken to complete the project or assignment. Specificity builds on the positive rather than talking abstractly about unmet potential.

One final comment on the topic of "potential": Have you reached yours? If so, congratulations! However, my guess is that *no one* actually believes that potential is an end point; rather, it's a constantly evolving benchmark that we strive throughout our lives to achieve. You might want to share this nugget of truth with your students, as well.

Summary

E. Paul Torrance, creator of the Torrance Tests of Creative Thinking and author of 88 books, had an intense interest in imaginative thinking. His interest began as a high school teacher, where he encountered many so-called problem students who did not want to complete their assigned work. Several years later, Torrance became a research psychologist in the Air Force Survival Training Program, learning time after time that although high intelligence was a common trait among his subjects, those with the highest survival skills had more abundant creativity and risk-taking behaviors. From there, Torrance's career studying creativity spanned several decades.

Commenting on his perceptions of what types of tasks underachievers should pursue, Torrance wrote, "Don't waste a lot of expensive energy in trying to do things for which you have little ability or love. Do what you can do well and do what you love, giving freely of the infinity of your greatest strengths and most intense loves" (Torrance, n.d., para. 3).

Throughout this chapter, I've presented several techniques and methods that students might use (often with an adult's help) to secure a worthwhile education. I hope these techniques are beneficial. Most important, though, is the attitude expressed through Torrance's view of the goals that underachievers should pursue—things they love and have the ability to accomplish. Indeed, such positive attention to the possibilities that lie within underachievers may be the greatest gift we can give to these students who are often recognized more for what they don't do or have not accomplished as opposed to the possibilities that lie within reach, if only we extend a hand of support.

6

Getting to *A*: Alternatives

E-mail messages from unknown recipients can be scary, especially if the single word in the subject line is *desperation* and a portion of the e-mail address itself contains the word *assassin*. Nonetheless, I opened this uninvited message to find this:

Dear Dr. Delisle:

I am an 18-year-old college freshman on the verge of dropping out. I was a constant daydreamer growing up and diagnosed with ADD. I got by easily in school but was labeled as an underachiever. But really, what can you achieve in an environment where you are not challenged and lose interest quickly? I was put on medication but stopped taking it. I felt there was nothing wrong with me and that if I could concentrate extremely well with things I liked, how could I have a problem with attention? I recently took an online IQ test and scored above 130. I know that's not as high as some kids you know, but it's still respectable.

I took a lot of self-identification tests online as well, try-ing to discover who I really am and why I'm having problems in school, maybe even what career to pursue. I don't know where to turn or what to do. School (even in my community college) teaches in small steps, and others not being able to see the big picture doesn't help me at all. I can't get by in college like I could earlier. I never studied in high school, and I don't know how to do it now.

I live in a rural area and am just looking for somewhere to go to discover who I really am and how I need to go about learning. Right now, I'm losing hope and slipping into depression; I can feel it. I don't want to feel like this. I've always been an optimist, but that's starting to fade. Please, can you give me the name of a psy-chologist near to where I live who specializes in people like me. I feel trapped and isolated from unleashing my true potential. I'm dying on the inside.

—Jacob

It would be hard enough to compose a cogent response to a poi-gnant letter such as this with someone I knew person-ally, but to try to be both comforting and helpful to a faraway cyberspace stranger is even more dif-ficult. Still, I tried, and via dozens of e-mails over the next few months, I suggested various strat-egies that Jacob might employ, including looking elsewhere for academic sustenance (he was self-medicating to get through his tedious classes) while simultaneously seeking counseling for his many valid concerns. He took both suggestions, scheduling two independent studies, in psychology and philosophy, with professors at a nearby university. Also, with the aid of a psychologist, Jacob focused on a career in nuclear mechanics, a program he gained admission to through the U.S. Armed Forces.

More than a decade later, Jacob and I are still in touch and, during a recent exchange, he offered this perspective on his earlier years:

> Since a very young age, I couldn't wait to be an adult so I would get the respect I thought I deserved. I was full of questions about life, not just the material they were supposed to teach me. I craved some adult connection and didn't get it, so I withdrew from reality, playing computer games and surfing Internet porn.
>
> What I was seeking was someone to engage me in thought. (A smart guidance counselor would have been nice . . .) Now, as a young adult, I seek out those who are intelligent and mature enough to question the most basic ideas we take for granted. I'm learning about life from the ground up and making mistakes that many people have made before me. Thank you for taking me seriously so many years ago, and still today.
>
> —Jacob

Jacob needed a lot of things all at once, but perhaps the most pressing issue for him was a need for *alternatives* that would allow him to find and pursue his passions. He felt stuck in an academic rut from a very young age, and this led to behaviors in adolescence that were injurious to his physical and mental health.

It's difficult to find hard data on how many Jacobs—kids who are very capable but feel stifled by restrictions in the curriculum— there are in our schools, but the evidence is there in far too many cases. High school student surveys dating back more than 20 years point to the general lack of relevance that Jacob found so pervasive in school. For example, in a 2000 report from the Organisation for Economic Co-operation and Development (OECD) that surveyed high school students in 32 countries, nearly half of all students worldwide reported that they were frequently bored in school. The United States percentage was 61 percent (OECD, 2000). In a survey of 467 high school dropouts for the Gates Foundation, nearly half said boredom was a major factor in their decision to leave school (Bridgeland, Dilulio, & Morison, 2006). In the respected National Survey of Student Engagement 2010 (Indiana University, 2010), 66 percent of 43,000 students reported being bored *every day* in school, and 81 percent of those students attributed boredom to uninteresting material. Further, 64 percent reported having to work hard in "none" or "1 or 2" classes. Lastly, in the 2015 Gallup annual survey of nearly 1 million public school students, only 50 percent of respondents reported being engaged in school.

These data point to a pernicious possibility: underachievement may be more pervasive in schools than we think it is. It is only when the Jacobs, Martys, and Sierras in our classrooms come to our full attention that we begin to take their academic plights seriously.

Alternative Strategy 1: Use the Past to Understand the Present

Sometimes, in order to move forward, we first have to glance back. Such is the case when we consider what education could look like if seen through the lens of a remarkable figure in world history: Leonardo da Vinci. In *How to Think Like Leonardo da Vinci* (Gelb, 2004), author Michael Gelb reviews the principles of da Vinci's life that made him into one of mankind's most prominent geniuses. Seeing da Vinci as a global archetype of human potential, Gelb categorizes seven ways that individuals can make their lives more creatively and intellectually fulfilling. The Italian names for these traits are as follows:

1. *Curiosita:* all-consuming curiosity
2. *Dimostrazione:* experiential learning/learning from mistakes
3. *Sensazione:* learning through all of the senses
4. *Sfumato:* accepting ambiguity as a part of learning

5. *Arte/Scienza:* interdisciplinary links between the two domains
6. *Corporalita:* physical well-being and nutrition
7. *Connessione:* interconnectedness of all things

Commenting on the importance of these qualities, and the frequent lack of attention paid to them in school, a 10th grader from Vancouver (Kris) reviews how each of them is "murdered" (her term) in her high school, resulting in a lack of appreciation for the very attributes that create genius. As she observes, "At every turn, schools and society are set on pushing back the most creative individuals. Their common traits are not welcomed nor encouraged and certainly not nurtured. This must not persist, because I think the world is long overdue for another da Vinci type right now" (Bradburn, 2007, para. 14).

Using Gelb's book as a resource, educators would be wise to do an inventory with students about the accessibility of each mode of learning that Gelb articulates. Use these attributes as a springboard for checking the relevance of learning that many underachievers—and others—crave to find in their education.

One nation where academic boredom doesn't seem to be as pervasive is Finland, which has recently become the poster child for excellence that all schools should seek to emulate. Personally, I'm not a bandwagon type of guy, as every paragon of excellence eventually falls from its pedestal and is replaced with the next best thing. Still, it's hard to argue against the many elements of a typical Finnish education. According to Darling-Hammond (2010), the not-so-surprising reasons that Finnish students jump to the global head of the class academically include the following:

- Curriculum focuses on broad-based, interdisciplinary themes and issues.
- Students engage in hands-on, authentic learning, using the tools, language, and processes associated with professionals in real-world settings.

- Students are given time during the school day to explore their interests and hobbies.
- Students are given autonomy in making choices about what to study.
- Small-group instruction in every classroom is common, based on students' academic needs and strengths.
- Students are involved in self-assessment and lesson planning.
- Teachers have great autonomy in choosing appropriate curriculum.
- High-stakes testing is not done.
- Weekly professional development is done in collaborative groups.

Perhaps one of the reasons these practices are successful is because these principles are based on an assumption of student and teacher competence. If teachers don't feel that their every decision is second guessed by a higher authority and if students believe that their teachers are flexible enough to allow individual expression to become a daily part of learning, then it is only natural that academic success is high and boredom is low. For students such as Jacob, whose underachievement is based on a lack of both rigor and relevance, elements typical of a Finnish education are those that are likely to entice them to give school another shot.

It's the teachers who really want to influence their students' lives and watch them succeed that make a difference. Teachers who connect with students on a personal level are the ones that inspire students like me to learn. After all, if a teacher doesn't seem to care, why should the student?

One needn't go to Finland, though, to find a personalized approach to learning that engages students to their cores. One such place where this occurs daily is The Roeper School, the first independent school in Michigan to admit African Americans on an equal basis to whites in the 1950s and the second independent school in the United States to focus exclusively on educating gifted children (starting in 1956). One of the school's founders, Annemarie Roeper, was a Holocaust survivor whose life was saved in great part to the heroic efforts of her soon-to-be husband, George. When they began their school in the United States in 1942, they did so with a philosophy undergirded by a belief in "global interdependence," a human interconnectedness and understanding that was never in evidence under the Nazi regime.

More than seven decades later, The Roeper School is still an intellectual and creative haven to the 600+ (preK through 12th grade) students who attend this gem. The Roeper School's unique philosophy is evident in its Educational Statement of Purpose:

> Our purpose is to guide students on the journey to becoming discerning, humane, engaged adults. . . . A Roeper education is characterized by outstanding and profound student-teacher relationships that foster mutual respect. When children are genuinely offered a voice from young ages, they grow to become adults who will do the same for others. This belief pervades every practice of the school. . . . We emphasize the importance of students doing their own thinking and making their own choices both in and out of the classroom, so that they become active stakeholders in their education and in their communities. . . . We hold process in equal regard with content and promote a nuanced understanding of subjects and a passion for learning. . . . The Roeper School offers a panoramic educational experience that reaches past the scope of college preparation and inspires individuals for life. (Roeper School Board of Trustees, 2013, paras. 1–5)

In most public school systems, the elected board of education members develop a mission statement and philosophy of education intended to serve as the foundation for what goes on daily in classrooms. Still, how many teachers even *know* the mission and philosophy of their school districts, and how many board of educa-tion members and school administrators focus on these statements as they evaluate the merits of daily instruction and student-teacher interaction? At a school like Roeper, a world in miniature is created: a "world that reflect(s) not only the racial and cultural diversity of the larger world but also the wonder, the failures, the confusion, the richness, the moral conundrums, the flashes of genius, the thrill of solitary discovery, and the profound satisfaction of a successful group achievement" (Ruff, 2016, p. 5).

Despite low grades and bad attitudes, the majority of students who do poorly on purpose seek something more from their educa-tion than a yearlong litany of basic assignments and disengaged interactions with educators. The kind of education provided at The Roeper School, the qualities that make Finnish schools so accommo-dating and successful, and the approaches to learning that created the genius of da Vinci are possible in your school. Not only will the education of students who underachieve be enhanced, but school will once again become a place that inspires everyone who enters its doors.

Alternative Strategy 2: Become Reacquainted with the Invitational Classroom

A quote that is commonly attributed to Haim Ginott seems appro-priate here:

I've come to a frightening conclusion that I am the decisive ele-ment in the classroom. It's my personal approach that creates the climate. It's my daily mood that makes the weather. As a teacher, I possess a tremendous power to make a child's life miserable or joyous. I can be a tool of torture or an instrument of inspiration. I can humiliate or heal. In all situations, it is my response that decides whether a crisis will be escalated or de-escalated and a child humanized or dehumanized.

My son, Matt, missed out in 1st grade. His teacher was fine, but she wasn't Ms. Harris. When I would make the trek most afternoons to pick up Matt at school, I noted that Ms. Harris would do the same thing each day. She would get down to eye-level with her students and shake their hands, tussle their hair, give a splashy high-five, or do some other physical gesture as each of them left her classroom. Each gesture was accompanied by a message: "Great answer in math today, Tony" or "Thanks for helping me pass out papers, Laquisha."

Every student, every day—always a new message. Ms. Harris intrigued me.

I lingered one day, mentioning to Ms. Harris that I noticed how she ended each day as her students walked to their busses, and I asked why she did it. Her response?

"I don't know what happens when my students get home. Some have parents and snacks waiting, other kids have their own keys to let themselves in, and some don't go home at all—they head to daycare until 6:00 p.m. I have no control over any of this, but I *do* have control over their last minute of the day with me, and I want that memory to be a good one."

Indeed, Matt missed out.

Ms. Harris is what authors Purkey and Novak (1984) would call an "intentional inviter," which is one of four types of characters who inhabit every classroom. Invitational Education itself is defined as a "perceptually based, self-concept approach to the educative process and professional functioning that centers on four basic principles:

1. People are able, valuable, and responsible and should be treated accordingly.
2. Teaching should be a cooperative venture.
3. People possess untapped potential in all areas of human development.

4. This potential can best be realized in places, policies, and programs that are specifically designed to invite development." (p. 2)

In essence, all teachers have a choice in the types of classrooms they design. One option is to regard their classrooms as a factory in which students punch the clock precisely at 8:00 a.m., proceeding through an assembly line of subjects and pumping out academic widgets in unison until a bell rings and calls on them to make another form of widget in the next room. At 2:15, a dismissal siren will call an end to another workday.

Another option is to create an atmosphere that resembles a family —a place where discussion is frequent, individual preferences and differences are noted, errors are expected, and successes are lauded. It even looks more like a home than a school, with personal items displayed, bulletin boards in full bloom (yes, even in high schools), and quiet corners for individual reflection time.

> I want to learn from someone who *wants* to teach it, not because they feel like they have to. Teachers should be or try to be passionate about what they're teaching. That helps me to learn more.

Using both research and anecdotes as evidence of the benefit of the family approach, Purkey and Novak conclude that students' perceptions of themselves are frequently derived from their teachers' perceptions of them. Therefore, this self-concept approach to learning and teaching is based on the premise that if teachers can convince their students that they are capable, then students are more likely to act in competent ways.

That kind of makes sense, doesn't it?

This is an especially effective approach to use with the types of students who are the subjects of this book—underachievers and selective consumers—both of whom thrive when the relationship aspect of schooling is paramount in teachers' minds.

Purkey and Novak (1984) classify educators into four camps:

1. Intentional inviters
2. Unintentional inviters
3. Intentional disinviters
4. Unintentional disinviters

Here are some examples of each.

The intentional inviter is a teacher who is able to link theory and practice, realizing that behavior is somewhat predictable if you know each student personally. They understand that school is only one part of their students' lives, and they strive to be open-minded about how a bad evening at home can presage a foul mood in class the following day (for both teachers and students!). Their use of humor can be self-deprecating but is never harsh or directed at students, and they remind students frequently and genuinely of their value and individuality. Ms. Harris, the 1st grade teacher cited earlier, is an example of an intentional inviter. She knows what she's doing and why she does it, and she reflects on the effect of her actions.

The unintentional inviter "seems to have stumbled into particular ways of functioning that are usually effective, but they have a difficult time explaining why" (Purkey & Novak, 1984, p. 18). Consistency is not their forte, and they often rely on gut instinct or past experiences that have worked as their modus operandi for classroom management. Flying by the seat of their pants often works for them. They regard teaching as a very human enterprise and seem to have natural gifts to engage students and make them feel welcomed. But if their downfall comes, and their best-laid instructional plans fall apart, they are often not reflective enough to analyze why their usual approach was not a success this time around. When working with underachievers, unintentionally inviting teachers might wonder why a strategy that worked with Eddie last year doesn't work with Jennifer this year. They would be wise to internalize the wisdom of creativity researcher Donald MacKinnon (1978) who wrote, "The same fire that melts the butter hardens the egg" (p. 17).

Intentional disinviters are teachers who should never work with anything organic, especially children. Their actions, behaviors, demeanors, and language all seem intended to bring out the worst in people. If a smart student messes up one day, the out-loud message that is likely to be sent goes something like this: "Oops! I guess Little-Miss-Perfect isn't so perfect after all!" Likewise, if a typically misbehaving or uncooperative student is having an especially good day, an intentional disinviter will say something like "If you acted this way more often, perhaps other kids would want to work with you sometimes." Intentionally disinviting teachers are rare but not yet extinct. Soon, hopefully.

Unintentional disinviters send messages they believe are positive and affirming, but the intended audience doesn't generally agree. For example, in an attempt to laud a student's success, a teacher might say, "There was only one *A* on this quiz. Can anyone guess who got it?" Another example comes from a high school student who was attempting an accelerated math class for the first time. Here's his recollection: "My grades were adequate, but I hated the pressure. For example, the seating was rearranged after every test, with the highest average in the right front and the lowest in the left rear" (Cox, Daniel, & Boston, 1985, p. 48). I have to assume the teacher who devised this classroom tango of a seating plan thought it would reward the students in the front and pump up the ones in the rear to buckle down and study. However, I doubt those goals were actually achieved.

Generally speaking, no one person is likely to be any one of these types all the time, although the hope is that intentionally inviting teachers would serve us better than the other categories of educators. Purkey and Novak provide a substantial glossary of simple things everyone in a school can do to become more intentionally inviting—from teachers to secretaries to counselors to cafeteria workers:

- Have a giveaway library of books or CDs.
- Hang live plants.
- Change bulletin boards regularly.
- Ask how students got their first names.
- Tell your students when they taught you something you didn't know.
- Grade student papers in green ink, not red.
- At the end of a unit, survey students for what worked and what didn't.

Purkey and Novak's work is gaining a resurgence as we now look at student engagement as one of the primary motivators to their academic growth. It's not a new concept, just one that was summarily discarded for a while in the manic quest for student performance indicators based on numbers alone. The best teachers, though—those intentional inviters—never abandoned the principles that made their classrooms resemble families more than factories. For selective consumers, especially, this return to student engagement is a welcome return to an education based on relationships, not regurgitation.

Alternative Strategy 3a: Refocus Attention on Both In- and Out-of-School Options

The last thing many educators would ever consider doing is putting capable students who do not perform well academically into advanced classes. For reasons based both on punishment ("You have to *earn* your right into AP courses") and instructional legitimacy ("If she's not doing well in basic math, wouldn't she be even more frustrated in advanced algebra?"), teachers often keep underachievers out of the very course options that might ignite their interest in learning. In addition, countless parents of underachieving students have told me that they'd rather have their smart son or daughter fail a hard class than an easy one. Their rationale? Maybe they'll pick up some new content, even if it's not reflected in their final grades.

> For me, I like to see and make that real-world application. I like to not just learn something but learn how it will relate to my future.

These perceptions are born out in a classic study of 10 gifted underachieving high school students. Linda Emerick (1992) investigated the factors that these 10 students found most beneficial to the eventual reversal of their weak academic performance. Although external influences played a role (e.g., extracurricular activities, personal interests, parental involvement), the in-school factors that were most influential in turning these academic wallflowers into high achievers included the following:

- Taking advanced courses that were more "fun" (i.e., more complex).
- Having some choice in both curriculum and project selection to show competence.
- Engaging in discussion-based classes where their opinions were valued by both the teacher and classmates.
- Minimizing traditional grading in lieu of more holistic methods of evaluation that also encouraged feedback and revision.

In essence, the least restrictive environment—one that assumes that even students who do not have a stellar history of academic performance are capable of high achievement—was the elixir that proved most successful in the lives of these 10 students. For educators brave enough to take this study to heart, there are many opportunities for smart students who underachieve to engage with more complex content.

Alternative Strategy 3b:
International Baccalaureate Program

In 1948, Marie-Therese Maurette was commissioned by UNESCO to write a handbook to help students become more globally aware and socially conscious (International Baccalaureate, n.d.). Her resulting publication eventually became the bedrock of the International Baccalaureate (IB) program offered at the International School of Geneva. It was a course of study for students ages 16–19 whose families moved frequently. The original intent of the IB program was to design a curriculum that followed students wherever they might move around the world, ensuring (it was hoped) that the more common the curriculum, the fewer gaps students would encounter in their educations. This humble beginning in Geneva eventually grew into a global phenomenon. What was once a high school program focused exclusively on children of diplomats and globetrotters, the IB program now exists in 146 countries and includes students ages 3–19, many of whom never travel at all.

The IB mission statement notes that the program is designed to "develop inquiring, knowledgeable, and caring young people who help to create a better and more peaceful world through intercultural understanding and respect" (International Baccalaureate, n.d, para. 5). Among the learner attributes that are encouraged in classroom activities and lessons are those that help students become more confident, curious, independent, empathetic, enthusiastic, and committed. If you notice, these are similar to the ways of learning that Michael Gelb (2004) identified as hallmarks of Leonardo da Vinci's education.

The integrated curriculum and thematic instruction that are part and parcel to IB are two reasons why this program is such an attractive option for many of the students whose words and lives have been on display in this book—smart individuals who underperform in school. For those students who are more vocationally inclined, a 2012 addition to the IB program is a career-related certificate, where career competencies and lifelong learning skills are emphasized.

Despite all of these positives, there are three caveats about IB that may make it less appealing to some. First, the initial cost of starting the program can run into the tens of thousands of dollars. Although expensive, this sum includes teacher training and on-site evaluation to ensure the IB precepts are followed. Indeed, the adoption of an IB program is not a small commitment to make. Second, some believe that the IB curriculum is too politically liberal, advocating for a global approach to education rather than a nationalistic, "our country first" approach. In some conservative school districts, an IB program may draw suspicion and raised eyebrows because of this emphasis. Third, if an IB program is adopted and students graduate from it, many colleges do not have a vehicle established to give those students credit for the work completed. With Advanced Placement (AP) courses (more on those later), colleges can match up which AP high school courses correlate with university offerings and award credits. This is harder to do with an IB program diploma.

Despite these criticisms, though, the IB option is one that offers much hope for students—underachieving or otherwise—who believe that education doesn't end with a high school or college diploma. Even if budgetary or other constraints prevent a district from instituting the entire IB program, there is nothing to stop individual teachers from checking out IB materials and determining ways to incorporate some of the strategies into their individual classroom curricula.

Alternative Strategy 3c: Advanced Placement (AP)

What was once rare is now becoming commonplace: the existence of AP courses in high schools. Initiated in 1955 after a three-year study that confirmed some high school seniors were capable of completing college-level work, AP courses are now available in three dozen subject areas, from U.S. History to Studio Art: 3D Design. Course content is determined by a panel of subject-area experts and college professors and is prescriptive by design, so an AP course in one school mirrors the same offering in another school. A standardized test is available at the end of each course and is scored on a 1–5 scale. Colleges generally accept scores of 3 or higher to earn credit. Nearly 90 percent of U.S. higher education institutions have policies regarding AP credit, making it a universally available program involving millions of students annually.

Although it is widely accepted, AP does have its critics. Some of those critics attest that students who take AP courses yet perform poorly on the AP exam do no better in college than students who didn't take any AP courses, which calls into question the merits of the curriculum as a whole (e.g., Sadler, Sonnert, Tai, & Klopfenstein, 2010). Further, some college professors assert that students who get college credit by scoring a 3 or 4 on the AP exam are not fully prepared for the subsequent courses they take in their particular disciplines. The issue of academic rigor also arises, as most high schools do not restrict access to AP courses to a particular segment of the student population. Therefore, any student who wishes to sign up for an AP course is allowed to do so (even if counseled *not* to do so by teachers or others). This raises the question of whether the AP course content is all that it purports to be, for if an AP class is composed of students of widely varying abilities, how can the advanced nature of the content and instruction be assured?

Despite its critics, AP is not only likely here to stay but also grow. Indeed, a recent addition to its roster is the AP Capstone program, an independent, research-based set of two courses (seminar and research) designed to "cultivate curious, independent, and collaborative scholars and prepare them to make logical, evidenced-based decisions" (College Board, 2017, para. 1). The AP Capstone program begins in 10th or 11th grade and is designed to build argument-based writing skills in students as they pursue a topic of interest—for example, whether issues of national security take precedence over an individual citizen's right to privacy. As students study their chosen topic, they build an argument and propose real-world solutions that are then communicated to various audiences. If, upon completion of the seminar and research courses, students score a 3 or higher on the respective AP exam, then they can combine this with scores of 3 or higher on four additional AP exams of their choosing to be awarded a capstone diploma. Approximately 650 schools currently offer the AP Capstone program, with additional high schools added annually.

This independent option (that is quite different from the less-flexible format of traditional AP courses) may quiet some critics who believe that AP is too didactic and prescriptive in design, but is an option like AP Capstone a good option for gifted students who underachieve? My experiences with such students in AP courses has been a mixed bag. Although many appreciate that the course content is advanced, the emphasis is generally placed more on coverage of content than on in-depth analysis of it—and depth is the very quality that gifted students who underachieve value most. AP Capstone is new enough that the jury is still out on whether it is a viable choice for students who clamor to do independent work but do not have a strong history of project completion. Time will tell, perhaps, if it offers promise for smart students who can achieve but often don't.

As ever, the most important and relevant factor in the eventual success of an underachieving student in an AP course is not the content but the teacher. Before suggesting or assigning a selective consumer or underachieving student to an AP course, it would be beneficial to sit down with the AP teacher, student, and someone (you, perhaps) who believes in this student's abilities but is unsure if the AP course is a good fit. This conversation, along with subsequent follow-up discussions, will be the best indicator of the worthiness of a particular AP option. The student-teacher dynamic, rather than the course itself, will most likely determine the degree of academic success the underachieving student can achieve.

Alternative Strategy 3d: Online Learning

When I went to school (which was, granted, so long ago that Earth was still in the process of cooling), the only options for additional learning outside the classroom were either summer camp, Scouts, or some other forms of extracurricular enrichment. Computers had not yet entered the scene, so the most sophisticated instruction available was generally an early Saturday morning TV show with a guy named John Gnagy trying to teach drawing. Other than that, learning was usually led by an adult trying to teach particular skills or subjects in real time.

Of course, things have changed dramatically in the years since I was growing up, right? Well, maybe not so much. "Within an hour's drive of the campuses of Google, Apple, Intel, Cisco, and many other companies that brought us the world of digital information we now inhabit, you would be hard-pressed to find a single school in which every student and teacher has 24/7 access to the tools that these companies have created" (Chen, 2010, p. 5).

This observation brings a stark reality into focus: there is a disconnect between the technological tools many of our students have at their personal disposal and the ones they are provided with at school. Teaching so-called 21st century learning skills may be a great goal in the abstract, but the reality of its existence continues to be spotty.

With that in mind, let's turn our attention to online learning and its powerful potential for engaging otherwise disengaged students. Let's start at the top: Khan Academy. Salman Khan was a young hedge fund manager who had two younger cousins who needed tutoring in math, but he found himself in a dilemma. He lived in Boston, and his cousins lived in New Orleans. It's tough to tutor long distance, so Khan decided to produce a video of some math lessons and placed it on YouTube for his cousins to view. They liked the video because they could view it at their leisure and rewatch it if they needed to repeat a particular concept they were still trying to comprehend. Soon, others took notice, and Khan's viewership expanded greatly. It grew so much, in fact, that Khan gave up his lucrative day job and began the nonprofit Khan Academy. Today, more than 1 million people every month access thousands of videos available on countless topics. What began as a one-man operation to help family has grown into a global phenomenon with hundreds of presenters offering instruction.

In reviewing Khan Academy, Barbara Branch (2012) stated that it "opens a revolutionary discussion of the approach to teaching and learning. . . . It should be used as a resource and supplement for a curriculum that also includes problem solving and concept development" (p. 39). Given their accessibility and the variety of topics, Khan Academy videos can be used with kids turned off to traditional approaches to learning in the following ways:

- Since the videos are self-paced, they can be used in lieu of or as a supplement to classroom instruction where students already have a basic understanding of the topic under review.
- The videos can be used as homework or enrichment, cutting down on the amount of time individual teachers and students need to spend on topics with which students already have some content knowledge.
- The videos can be a safe way for students who underachieve to review concepts with which they have a passing familiarity but still need additional practice to master. The private nature of the videos—you watch them whenever you want—doesn't put underachieving students' lack of knowledge about a particular topic on display.

The universal availability of Khan Academy videos (in multiple languages) makes them a powerful vehicle for broadening a student's knowledge in countless topic areas. If educators are willing to give up some control of content and instruction, then the Khan Academy videos open the door to abundant options for engaging disengaged students. This may be a far-fetched thought, but couldn't groups of teachers develop assessments of particular videos' content, using these assessments to measure students' gained knowledge? Using the videos and teacher-designed assessment tools as conduits to determine students' knowledge might seem revolutionary today, but the promise such a plan holds for regaining the interest of students who have dismissed typical schooling as obsolete is worth testing the waters, is it not?

Another entertaining and informative option that has taken the world by storm are TED Talks. TED stands for technology, entertainment, and design, and the lecture series is the brainchild of creator Richard Saul Wurman who saw how these three elements could coalesce in synergistic fashion to create something bigger than their individual parts. In the early 1980s, he sponsored an invitation-only conference where the latest inventions were displayed—a Sony compact disc and 3D movie graphics created by George Lucas. Wurman then showed how these two inventions could be used together to map coastlines, thanks to another new discovery on the use of fractals by mathematician Benoit Mandelbrot.

Happily, this initial venture into the world of tomorrow took on a decidedly more consumer-friendly vibe a few years later. When TED reemerged in 1990, it did so as an annual conference held in Monterey, California, for people who were "united by their curiosity and open-mindedness—and also by their shared discovery of an exciting secret" (TED, n.d., para. 2). The rich and famous were invited to give presentations of 20 minutes or less, and as the TED phenomenon continued to grow, lesser-known individuals, including children and teenagers, became the stars of the show. Today, there are more than 1,000 TED Talks available, including the following:

- "Do Schools Kill Creativity?" by Sir Ken Robinson, which has almost 50 million hits and is the most popular TED Talk of all time.

- "The Power of Vulnerability" by Brené Brown, which examines the connections between people that make them able to empathize, belong, and love.
- "How I Held My Breath for 17 Minutes" by magician David Blaine (don't try this at home!).
- "A Promising Test for Pancreatic Cancer . . . from a Teenager" by Jack Andraka, a 16-year-old scientist who discovered a successful early detection test for pancreatic cancer.
- "A Teen Just Trying to Figure It Out" by Tavi Gevinson, a 15-year-old website designer who developed the popular web magazine *Rookie* for teenage girls seeking female role models to emulate.

Whatever the topic, there is likely a TED Talk that covers it, and the audiences who view the talks do so at no cost. So how can TED Talks be used with students who underachieve? They're certainly not a curriculum, and the short videos generally present a cursory description of whatever topic is covered.

Actually, the brevity of the videos is one of their biggest assets. Students who underachieve often like to take a taste of something before they dig in fully. Therefore, if a student is turned on to a particular topic he or she saw on a TED Talk, it could be the catalyst for a larger investigation that includes additional and more extensive research. As an independent study option with a teacher who is willing to try, TED Talks might just be the appealing appetizer to a grand buffet of learning.

> Good grades should not be all that school is about. If we learn how to learn and enjoy doing it, then good grades will come along, too.

An increasingly popular (and available) option to convince underachieving students of the benefits of schooling is a trend that actually began in 1929 at the University of Nebraska: the virtual high school. Of course, during the Great Depression, there was no technology that allowed students to communicate with teachers and professors electronically, but there was another option: the U.S. Postal Service. In order to serve the many isolated rural communities throughout Nebraska that were not large enough to offer a robust selection of advanced high school courses, the Independent Study High School (ISHS) was born.

If an advanced student in Ogallala, Nebraska, wished to learn physics or calculus but was unable to find a course at the local high school, ISHS would set up a correspondence course where learning materials and tests were sent by mail to a teacher in Ogallala willing to monitor that student's progress. Once completed, the assignments were mailed back to ISHS where they were evaluated by appropriately knowledgeable teachers. If students passed the course, then they earned high school credit for it. In fact, both then and now, students can receive an ISHS diploma without ever having stepped foot on the campus of the University of Nebraska, where ISHS is located. Now known as the University of Nebraska High School, the school is still operating and serves students in all 50 states and more than 135 nations. Their groundbreaking work continues.

According to a 2016 report, there were 447 virtual academies in the United States serving more than 262,000 students during the 2013–14 school year, with an average enrollment of 1,166 students in privately managed schools and 350 in publicly supported virtual schools (Miron & Gulosino, 2016). Class size was high, and each teacher was assigned 30–40 students.

The question of accountability was also addressed in this report. The virtual academies did not, as a whole, fare well, as they reported substantially weaker student performance indicators than did brick-and-mortar schools. To aid parents (and others) in the selection of a high-quality virtual school, an organization known as Best College Reviews (www.bestcollegereviews.org) analyzed virtual academies using the following metrics: affordability, number of courses offered, types of courses offered, and support services available for enrolled students. Their 2016–17 review lists the top 25 virtual schools, which includes

#1. Laurel Springs School

#2. Brigham Young University Independent Study

#3. University of Nebraska High School

#5. North Dakota Center for Distance Education

#9. Advantage School International

Are virtual academies a good option for students who underachieve? There are two schools of thought on this. According to Tynan-Wood (2016), students who are most successful in virtual schools are those who are self-motivated, are technologically savvy, and have a record of being responsible. Using these criteria, students who underachieve might be poor candidates for an independent approach to learning. However, there are others who contend that if a typical school situation is not producing results for underachieving students, what's the harm in trying a different approach? After all, the learning is self-paced, and the content courses may be selected according to student interest. If such an option prevents even one student from dropping out of school entirely, then the gamble is worth the risk.

Like any new venture, testing the waters is preferable to diving in full force, so beginning with one course in an area of high student interest is perhaps the best advice to follow. It's much better to succeed on a small scale than to fail spectacularly.

Clearly, the number of alternative options for students who perform poorly in school has never been larger or broader. The biggest barrier, in fact, might be one of attitude. There are plenty of people who want to hold back innovation until the underachieving student "bucks up" and starts showing some initiative and academic progress. Since this attitude has led to little success in the past, I hold out no hope that it will succeed in the future. It's time to change our paradigm when it comes to serving smart students who do poorly in school.

Summary

Early in this chapter, I recommended *How to Think Like Leonardo da Vinci* (Gelb, 2004) as a source for instructional and creative ideas to use with students who underachieve. In his conclusion to that book, Gelb writes, "The essence of Leonardo's legacy is the inspiration for wisdom and light to triumph over fear and darkness. . . . In an age of specialization and fragmentation, Leonardo da Vinci shines forth as a beacon of wholeness" (p. 259).

In reading this quote, my thoughts go back to Jacob, the young man whose letter opened this chapter. What he wanted—indeed, what he *needed*—more than an appropriate curriculum was an adult who believed he had within him more future possibilities than past disappointments. As da Vinci himself said, "Tears come from the heart, not from the brain."

By providing students such as Jacob with the personal guidance offered at a school with a philosophy that mirrors the one at The Roeper School, by allowing them to cut corners for the sake of learning something truly meaningful, and by giving them an opportunity to succeed in an independent manner usually reserved for the highest achievers, we are emboldening students who underachieve and preparing them for future success. As teachers, we must believe in these students more than they believe in themselves.

7

Getting to *A*: Aspirations

The following essay, written by a young woman about her personal underachievement, might seem a bit odd. After all, Elizabeth graduated as valedictorian, was a member of just about every club her high school offered, and earned multiple ribbons and trophies that document her academic prowess. Still . . . something was missing.

> In the pit of my stomach, I have a deep sense of unaccomplishment. Despite the armful of awards that seem to shout *model student*, I know the truth—I had never written a paper any earlier than the night before it was due, and "studying" for me consisted of cracking open the textbook only two or three times a semester. The glowing sense of victory I had always expected to show up at my high school graduation had stood me up. (Galbraith & Delisle, 2011, p. 122)

Elizabeth goes on to document one reason for the pervasive disappointment she felt about her high school experience:

My social studies teacher walked into the room, clapping his hands brusquely. "Okay, class, we have three weeks until the end of the school year and 10 chapters to cover. Turn to the section on the Korean War."

We opened our books.

"All right, now raise your right hand and place it palm down over the first page."

We looked around at one another, confused, but followed his instructions. "Now, we've *covered* it," said the teacher, his chins jiggling at the pun. "Let's move on."

"We're not going to learn about the Korean War?" protested one student.

"You don't need to know about the Korean War unless you're Korean."

A hand shot up in the back of the room. "I'm Korean."

"Oh . . . well, you can read that chapter on your own."

Unfortunately, this was the norm rather than the exception for a great chunk of my time in school. (Galbraith & Delisle, 2011, p. 123)

This story reveals an important caveat about underachievement: sometimes it's not the student who underachieves but the learning environment itself. I've never been a "teacher basher"—that academic pundit who sits back and complains about educators who do a lousy job in an enterprise I'm too intimidated to try myself—yet it's hard to argue that this student's disappointment with her high school education wasn't warranted.

Every student with whom I've worked in my 40 years of teaching, from the ones who struggled to learn simple concepts to the brightest stars in the academic universe, had aspirations to be more tomorrow than they are today. They wanted to be smarter, better looking, more popular, or simply happier. As teachers—as people—we ignore this reality at our peril, for it surely applies to us as much as it applies to our students. It might take a new perspective to consider that even those students who do poorly on purpose really do want to succeed in some capacity, but they do. As I've emphasized throughout this book, it's against human nature to want to fail, to look incapable or silly, or to seek out personal embarrassment.

In this chapter, we'll consider some ways to tap into the unrealized aspirations of some of our most challenging students. Perhaps we can rely on Ralph Waldo Emerson for guidance, as he wrote in 1883:

It is not for you to choose what he shall know, what he shall do. It is chosen and foreordained, and he only holds the key to his own secret. By your tampering and thwarting and too much governing, he may be hindered from his end and kept out of his own. (Emerson, 1883, para. 29)

Despite the sexist language of the time, Emerson's sentiment rang true then, and it still does today.

Aspirations Strategy 1: Learn the Benefits of Biblio- and Film Therapies

Books and movies are entertaining and informative. Through them, we can go places we've never been and meet people we'd otherwise not know. They allow us to escape, even if only for a little while. They can be entertaining, informative, and life-changing. By experiencing life through the written words or cinematic lenses of others, we can learn more about ourselves.

Bibliotherapy has been around for a while. Indeed, inscribed on the walls of Egypt's ancient library in Alexandria were the words *the nourishment of the soul*. With bibliotherapy, individuals gain insight into themselves by reading about the lives of others, whether actual people or fictional characters. Literature and stories can become a source of social and emotional guidance, as well as therapeutic tools for coming to terms with some of life's challenges. Film therapy is an updated take on bibliotherapy, but it ultimately has the same aim: self-understanding by experiencing the lives of others (via film and video).

For many students, these two therapies offer many benefits. Why? Memorable characters in literature and film are seldom boring. They have dreams, goals, aspirations, quirks, and unique qualities that make us want to learn more about them. If they don't, then we're liable to put the book back on the shelf or turn off the movie. As mentioned in Chapter 1, in *The Breakfast Club*, we are introduced to every high school student stereotype that exists. In *October Sky*, we watch a group of poor kids from Coalwood, West Virginia, turn their collective dream to become "rocket boys" into reality. In *The Curious Incident of the Dog in the Night-Time,* we meet a 15-year-old gifted boy with autism whose mission is to find the killer of a neighborhood dog. In *Matilda*, we meet a gifted young girl whose wits and ingenuity turn the tables on the evil Headmistress Trunchbull. Interwoven throughout each story's plot are many of the elements that real people face every day: conflict, hope, disappointment, triumph, and defeat. By interacting with a particular movie or book and inviting students to explore the connections between themselves and the characters they meet, we open the door for communication and understanding that isn't typically available through textbooks.

In 6th grade, I had a teacher who enjoyed pointing out my flaws. When I returned to school after a family death, he told me that I would never catch up and should go back to a basic math class. I felt so discouraged that I would never be able to catch up or be smart.

Thankfully, there are many resources that will help you chart this course. Judy Halsted's *Some of My Best Friends Are Books* (2009) highlights titles that will engage students from preschool through high school in virtually every genre—literature, poetry, science fiction, folktales, and more. Halsted also includes an informative guide for ways to discuss the benefits of bibliotherapy with students. Mensa International has also compiled an exhaustive selection of resources for their Mensa for Kids' Excellence in Reading program (available at www.mensaforkids.org/achieve/excellence-in-reading). Hundreds of titles are included, including Lois Lowry's *The Giver*, Johanna Reiss's *The Upstairs Room*, Pearl Buck's *The Good Earth*, and Ralph Ellison's *Invisible Man*.

Hebert (2006) compiled a list of school-appropriate films for use with students, including *Amazing Grace and Chuck,* about a kid who refuses to pitch for his baseball team until nuclear weapons are banned, a cause taken up later by professional ball players; *Lucas,* the story of a quirky, eccentric middle school kid whose journey of self-discovery includes many unexpected paths; and *Mona Lisa Smile,* the tale of a female college professor who is chastised by her colleagues for wanting to teach her students to think critically about art rather than just memorize who painted what. Some more contemporary movies include *The Perks of Being a Wallflower,* in which a socially awkward teen achieves his dreams with the help of two charismatic friends and a teacher; *Moana,* in which a teen girl sets out on a mission to save her people and is guided by a mentor who helps her through triumphs and setbacks to discover her own identity; *August Rush,* a drama with fairy tale elements in which a young, orphaned musical prodigy uses his gift to locate his birth parents;

and *Freedom Writers*, the true story of an inner-city teacher who takes a group of underachieving high school students and turns them into powerful wordsmiths.

These films, whether contemporary or more "vintage," carry a quality of hope. The central characters must battle demons, both internal and external, to arrive at places where they feel successful and emboldened. Even the older films, despite the sometimes-dated clothing and hairstyles, reveal issues and conflicts that are contemporary and relevant. Whatever their age, these films foster an awareness of the universality of certain human conditions and common aspirations that people have always strived to reach.

Aspirations Strategy 2: Introduce Students to Psychosynthesis

Each summer for the past five years, I have spent a week camping with 70 highly gifted 10–17 year olds in the mosquito-shrouded forests of Michigan. Our first scheduled activity of each day is a 90-minute session of psychosynthesis, a term and procedure I knew nothing about until becoming a counselor at this camp. When I thought about doing an activity of this length, daily, with 10 kids of mixed ages, I questioned whether this camp counseling thing was such a good idea. As it turned out, psychosynthesis has become a favorite daily activity, for both my young campers and me, and has also become an activity I do regularly during the school year with my 9th graders.

Psychosynthesis was developed by Italian psychiatrist Roberto Assagioli (1888–1974). The procedure is designed to bring balance and integration—synthesis—to oneself through a series of guided visualizations. Thanks to a series of convenient coincidences, Piero Ferrucci came to work with Assagioli in Florence, Italy. After his mentor's death, Ferrucci published a book, *What We May Be* (1982), that elaborates in exquisite detail on the purposes and benefits of psychosynthesis, along with numerous guided imagery exercises that can be used with both children and adults. Ferrucci explained the rationale for these exercises thusly:

> When it is balanced and healthy, human growth proceeds in all directions: it looks like an expanding sphere rather than a straight line. It is for precisely this reason that psychosynthesis endeavors to take into consideration all the dimensions of human life which truly matter and which, if left unacknowledged, lead to a fragmented, even absurd existence. (1982, p. 26)

Ferrucci then identifed the specific purposes of his psychosynthesis scenarios:

- The emergence of will and self-determination.
- The sharpening of the mind.
- The enjoyment of beauty.
- The enrichment of imagination.
- The awakening of the intuition.
- The realization of love.
- The discovery of the self and its purpose. (Ferrucci, 1982, pp. 26–27)

I'm sure many of you think this process is beyond the realm of a teacher's responsibilities or capabilities, describing something that resembles a séance more than it does a science class. That's what I believed, too, before I began conducting these exercises not only at camp but also, as mentioned, with my own gifted 9th graders. These highly capable kids are also highly stressed much of the time due to an academic workload that includes both AP and college classes. (Yes, even as 9th graders, my students take AP and dual-enrollment college courses.) The brief (5–10 minute) exercises, done with the lights off and with the students comfortably seated or lying on the floor, add a quiet end to any robust lesson. When I ring a chime at the end of the visualization exercise, students slowly sit up or return to their seats, often with eyes still half-closed and a smiling expression. Psychosynthesis has worked its charm in as little as 10 minutes. Imagine what it does each day at camp, with 90 minutes allotted to this mind-opening experience.

Each visualization exercise begins the same way, with the leader reciting the words of Buddhist monk Thich Nhat Hanh (1992, p. 10):

> Breathing in, I calm my body.
> Breathing out, I smile.
> Dwelling in the present moment,
> I know this is a wonderful moment.

After 30 seconds, the words are repeated, followed by one of many exercises that might have you visualize the environment around you or meet a mentor who will teach you everything you want to know about a subject of your choosing. Other exercises are more sensory in nature, such as shooting an arrow at an intended target, sailing a ship toward a destination you've been before or would like to visit, or watching a butterfly emerge from its chrysalis.

Psychosynthesis seems to be the ancestral forefather to one of education's most current prescriptions for good mental health: mindfulness. Practiced regularly, mindfulness exercises have been shown to increase empathy, reduce anxiety and impulse control, and increase concentration and GRE scores of college students (e.g., Lieberman, 2012; Mrazek, Franklin, Phillips, Baird, & Schooler, 2013). Resources abound, online and in print, for educators who wish to include mindfulness exercises into their repertoire of techniques to reach kids who often find themselves at odds with themselves—with either too many thoughts or not enough time to focus on positives or personal possibilities. Whichever approach you use, the overworked but underperforming students in your lives may benefit immensely by this curricular detour into the realm of psychosynthesis.

By the way, the name of the camp where I work each summer is Camp Yunasa. The term *yunasa* is the Lakota Sioux word for "balance." How appropriate is *that*?

Aspirations Strategy 3:
Explore with Students: "What Do I Want to Be When I Grow Up?"

The online survey of more than 6,000 gifted children, teens, and adults I referenced earlier included dozens of questions about life, school, passions, and friendships (Schultz & Delisle, 2013). One of the inquiries regarding future career options yielded the expected responses—college, professional occupation, something "interesting and lucrative"—as well as more than a few responses such as these:

- I have so many interests that I've compiled a list of things I *don't* want to be instead of the list of things I *do* want to be, because that list is shorter. (boy, age 14)
- I'm not sure what I want to major in yet, perhaps law or engineering or aerospace technology. Or perhaps elementary education. (girl, age 15)
- Right now, I want to be a bone doctor or a journalist. It's funny that there is hardly any relation between the two, yet I still want to be both. (boy, age 14)

These three kids are among the many gifted students, including those who underachieve, who are blessed (or cursed, depending on your perspective) with a particular condition called multipotential, which is defined as "the interest and ability to succeed in so many vocational areas that choosing one career path becomes problematic" (Delisle, 1992, p. 150.) The term itself came about via the Research and Guidance Laboratory for Superior Students (RGLSS), which began at the University of Wisconsin in 1957. Over the course of its decades-long existence, RGLSS saw thousands of gifted high school students who were interviewed and surveyed on numerous occasions. One issue that arose frequently with these gifted teens was the difficulty they faced in choosing a career path. As one adolescent put it, "Nothing is so simple for me that I can do a perfect job without effort, but nothing is so hard that I cannot do it. This is why I find it so difficult to decide my place in the future" (Hoyt & Hebeler, 1974, p. 12).

> In 7th and 8th grades, I was in Chorus. Whenever we hit the notes in a specific song, the amount of joy and energy that burst out of our teacher would transfer to me. Now understand . . . I cannot sing well, but this teacher made me feel I could do anything with the right amount of effort and support.

This ambivalence about one's career selection might seem to be an embarrassment of riches to some. After all, isn't it merely a problem of privilege to have so many options open to you that your biggest issue is which golden ticket to take? The truth is that it's anything but, and here's an analogy to prove it. Imagine you're at the best buffet in Las Vegas. Literally hundreds of mouthwatering choices await you and, as you scan the various salads, entrees, and desserts, you can't wait to make your selections and dig in.

That's when the waiter comes up to you and informs you of this buffet's unique rule: you can take as much as you'd like . . . of any one item. You protest, of course, mentioning that the purpose of a buffet is to have a smidgen of this and a dollop of that. Nevertheless, rules are rules, and this buffet strictly limits you to as much as you'd like of a single item. You might as well have eaten at home and saved $40.

This buffet dilemma is minor in comparison to the choices that gifted adolescents are asked to make as they decide college majors and career options. Add to this the rampant belief held by many school counselors and parents that gifted students should choose a career that befits their high intellects *and* that they should know at 18 years old what they want to be doing at 40. Doctor, lawyer, engineer, they're all fine. But creative writer, carpenter, or zombie make-up artist? Sorry, those just don't fit the model. They're too bizarre, basic, or "not gifted enough." If you're an underachieving student whom many believe is already "wasting your potential," there is the added stress of being told that low high school grades will likely limit your career options and doom you to a job that will be unsatisfying from the get-go.

Given the realities of being multipotential and the rabid college and career expectations held by many adults about gifted adolescents' futures, it is essential to have conversations about these topics and provide early and frequent career guidance to our most capable students. Such career exposure is commonplace for students whose future goals may not include college, but when it comes to high-ability students, such exposure is generally limited or altogether absent. Sadly, of all of the issues confronting gifted teens, the area that gets the least amount of focus is the one that most of them desperately seek: What happens after high school ends?

Here are some ideas and resources to get you started.

Listen to commencement speeches. Many of these ceremonial speeches are forgotten even before they are completed. Most consist of a collection of verbal bromides that harangue students to "be true to yourself" and "always try to do your best"—advice that is so obvious that it should be left unstated. However, there are other commencement addresses that even cause ready-to-party graduates to sit up and listen. Annually, these top 10 or 15 high school and college commencement speeches are compiled by news outlets such as *Time, USA Today, The Huffington Post*, and National Public Radio, which has the distinction of also listing the top commencement speeches of all time, going as far back as 1774.

Four personal favorites of mine are these:

- Steve Jobs, in his 2005 commencement speech at Stanford University, offered the following advice: "Don't let the noise of others' opinions drown out your own inner voice. . . . Stay hungry. Stay foolish."

- Facebook COO Sheryl Sandberg spoke at the University of California, Berkeley, in 2016, shortly after the sudden death of her husband. In her speech, she acknowledges the glaring irony that her husband's death helped her appreciate life, as she now focuses every day on the little moments of joy instead of reliving a long list of mistakes made.
- Thomas Friedman's 2005 address at Williams College included this advice: "Whatever you plan to do, whether you plan to travel the world next year, go to graduate school, join the workforce, or take some time off to think, don't just listen to your head, listen to your heart. It is the best career counselor there is."
- Oprah Winfrey, in her 2017 commencement address at Agnes Scott College, offered this advice: "You're nothing if you're not the truth. I've made a living, I've made a life—I've made a fortune, really—from being true to myself. . . . Those of you who have a lot of shoes know having a closet full of shoes doesn't fill up your life. Living a life of substance can. Substance through your service."

After reading Friedman's speech and commenting on elements with which he could personally identify, one of my 9th graders wrote, "The only thing worse than being denied opportunities is being forced to take them." Sage advice from a talented teen whose path to adulthood is just beginning.

Find these speeches, share them with your students, and wallow in the wisdom that can be encapsulated in even the briefest of commencement remarks.

Connect adolescents to people who love what they do. For more than a decade, I coordinated a gifted program at a middle school in Ohio. I had a budget of $0 and approximately 80 7th and 8th graders to serve. One thing I did have was access to a school bus and driver two days a month. Scanning the Cleveland area for free places to go, we explored many venues, including the Federal

Reserve Bank, Akron Children's Hospital's Neonatal ICU, an Amish school, the Haven of Rest homeless shelter, and the Liquid Crystal Institute at Kent State University. In each of our day-long excursions, my students interacted with people who absolutely loved what they did, whether it was providing guidance to a newly homeless family or nursing a premature baby to health.

When we returned to school, after spending the day with scientists, artists, doctors, teachers, medical students, or economists, the question students had to answer was not what they learned that day but what they learned about *themselves*. This form of informal career guidance gave my students incredible insight into the options that awaited them in just a few short years.

Of course, this exposure to career possibilities in middle school could lead to a more long-lasting mentorship as students get older. Whether done as a summer internship, a for-credit independent study course run through the student's high school, or simply a shadowing experience arranged informally through a parent or adult friend, the idea of getting multipotential teens into an occupation that looks interesting from the outside is the best way to determine if it looks equally good from the inside.

Connect students to their "near peers." One of the places my 7th graders visited was just a walk away: our town's high school. At the school's entrance, my students were greeted by a National Honor Society high school senior. After some quick introductions and snacks, each 7th grader followed his or her assigned "mentor" through the day's schedule. Whether it was AP Calculus, gym class, or study hall, each pair of students went together to these classes. Lunch was a special treat, as the 7th graders were seated with juniors and seniors, and *they* were the center of attention. At day's end, all 80 students were put together in a large open space, and I gave them this assignment:

"12th graders, what do you know now that you wish you knew when you were in middle school? And 7th graders, what questions do you have for these seniors—questions I am obviously too old to answer?"

The day ended with high-fives, hugs, and handshakes, but we weren't done yet. Each senior was required to handwrite a personal letter to his or her assigned 7th grader, which I delivered to the younger students when we next got together. One of my favorite letters was from Michael to Tim. Here's an excerpt:

Hey Tim! How's the rest of 7th grade going? I hope you enjoyed your time with me, and I can tell that you can't wait to take AP Physics. (ha, ha!)

Looking back on the past six years, I have only three pieces of advice: enjoy your time, as it goes faster than you think. Get involved in something . . . whatever it may be. Lastly, enjoy 8th grade, because you won't rule the school again until four years later, in your senior year.

I can tell you are intelligent and a little bit anxious, Tim. My advice: simply believe in yourself, even when it's hard to do so. Have a great school year's end, and I look forward to seeing you at the town pool this summer.

—Michael

To a 7th grader looking for guidance, 12th graders are the equivalent of gods and goddesses. These "near peers" are just enough older to have credibility, but they're not so old that their ideas are looked at with suspicion.

I set up this "near peer field trip" because I'd exhausted so many other community options. Little did I know that to most of my 7th graders, it was the most appreciated trip of them all. Career guidance for gifted adolescents isn't about selecting a college or job that is ideal for them. Rather, it is about looking at which options best fit their personalities, interests, and lifestyles, keeping in mind that they very likely will change their minds later. For gifted students who do poorly on academic tasks, this full-frontal exposure to the real-world of careers and possibilities broadens their horizons in ways both unexpected and beneficial. It also helps make multipotential less of a burden and more of an exciting and challenging set of options.

Talk about celebrity U-turns. As much as I don't like concentrating on fame that may be devoid of accomplishments, there are lessons to be learned from celebrities whose paths to success started out in wildly different places from where they began. For students who are unsure of the directions they wish to take, learning that people who made their marks in acting, business, writing, and other endeavors began elsewhere is valuable information to absorb. This might give them the courage to propel forward with the notion that they could backtrack later and still be successful. Here is a sample of famous folks who took U-turns on their road to notoriety:

- Ashley Judd majored in French and Classics at the University of Kentucky.
- Sean "Diddy" Combs majored in Business at Howard University.
- Conan O'Brien majored in American Literature and History at Harvard.
- Denzel Washington majored in Journalism and Drama at Fordham University.
- Mick Jagger majored in Economics at the London School of Economics.
- Gloria Estefan majored in Psychology at the University of Miami.
- J.K. Rowling majored in French and Classics at Exeter College.

These celebrity turn-arounds aren't isolated cases. In fact, if high school seniors enter college with a declared major, it usually doesn't last long. According to the National Center for Educational Statistics, approximately 80 percent of college freshmen eventually change their majors, and the average college student switches majors three times before landing on one that is a good fit (Snyder & Dillon, 2015). This may be reassuring news to those students who would love to major in "I Don't Know" but are discouraged from doing so by well-meaning adults trying to pigeonhole them into a career path for which they may not be ready.

In addition to these famous people who completed college with majors that were far different from what their celebrity status might suggest, there is another roster of well-known individuals who either never attended college or dropped out before completing a degree. They include Steve Jobs, Bill Gates, Richard Branson, Rachael Ray, Ellen DeGeneres, Mark Zuckerberg, Oprah Winfrey, and Lady Gaga. Going further back, you have people like Walt Disney, Benjamin Franklin, and Abraham Lincoln.

Sharing these anecdotes with your students is not meant to be an incentive for them to drop out or forego college altogether. It's simply a reminder of George Sands's quote that "It's never too late to be what you might have been."

Aspirations Strategy 4: Use Quotations to Better Understand Yourself

There is a special magic about a few well-stated *bon mots* that cause people to seek out quotations. But why are quotations often as influential as an entire book or speech? As with many things, the answer lies in the field of psychology. First, most quotations use precise and memorable language that evokes particular images that reflect our own lives or aspirations. Second, many quotes offer a form of emotional balm, a motivational force transferred from writer to reader. Third, when you find a quote that is personally relevant, the most common reaction is "Yes . . . exactly!" This identification with the words of a famous or unknown individual makes a connection that bonds together, even briefly, two people who will likely never meet.

Some teachers recognize students for high grades,
but not all students like that public attention.

With that in mind, it's not uncommon for schools to use quotes in various ways (in the hopes of reinforcing particular attributes in students). Sometimes, it's a quote of the day heard over morning announcements. Other times, classroom or hallway posters with quotes are displayed (e.g. "Mistakes are proof that you are trying," "It always seems impossible until it's done"). Then there are the ever-popular quotes that graduating seniors post alongside their yearbook photos.

My preference, though, is to dig a little deeper and use an activity that requires more personal identification with a quote. I begin by introducing students to some of my own favorite quotes, which I label as "quotes from the sages, quotes from the ages."

- "No person is your friend who demands your silence or denies your right to grow." —Alice Walker
- "The respect of others rights, is peace." —Benito Juarez
- "Feet, what do I need you for when I have wings to fly?" —Frida Kahlo
- "Birds sing after a storm, why shouldn't we?" —Rose Kennedy
- "You miss 100 percent of the shots you never take." —Wayne Gretzky
- "I always wanted to be somebody, but now I see I should have been more specific." —Lily Tomlin

After reading these quotes, I ask for personal interpretations and whether or not individual students can identify with the messages they impart. Next, I invite students to explore some of the many websites devoted to quotations. There are many, and each contains tens of thousands of school-appropriate quotes. Once students have had a chance to explore these sites, I ask them to identify one particular quote that has personal meaning and either write individually or discuss in small groups about the impact of those words.

Here is one example from a former 8th grader of mine, Lauren. Her quote, from an anonymous author, was this: "Someone once asked me, 'Why do you always insist on taking the hard road?', and I replied, 'Why do you assume I see two roads?'"

In the essay that followed, Lauren wrote about a school project she could have blown through carelessly, as her class average was high enough that it wouldn't have affected her overall grade.

"Yet I couldn't allow myself to do the easy thing," Lauren wrote. "I worked incredibly hard to make sure that my writing and presentation were the best they could be. . . . My friends were amazed that I had gone through all of that trouble for a class project. I couldn't explain it to them, but my conscience was satisfied and my inner honesty was intact."

Some might roll their eyes and tell Lauren to cut herself some slack, yet her personal devotion to excellence, even if it wasn't shared by every one of her classmates, is on full display in her essay.

For teens who are still riding the cusp of maturity, the use of quotes for self-reflection and understanding can become one more tool to use in reaching those who are not always attuned to classroom lessons. Be warned, though. You will have some students who select quotes for their shock value, wanting less to gain personal growth and more to seek laughter or chagrinned looks from classmates. Do not call these students out on their selections; rather, find a quote that *you* believe is indicative of their personalities or aspirations and share it with them privately. There is always a chance that you will create a quote convert.

Summary

Hans Reyersbach and his wife Margarete Waldstein were both *aspirational* and *inspirational* people. Better known as H.A. Rey and Margret Rey, they were the authors and illustrators of the *Curious*

George series. This pair of German Jews escaped the Nazi regime by riding bicycles that Hans had built himself from salvaged spare parts.

According to biographer Louise Borden (2005), their 11-day, 1,000-mile trek was done on the edge of danger. They could hear German bombs dropping as they pedaled through France, eventually arriving in Lisbon—a long stopover before they crossed the Atlantic to Brazil and, eventually, New York City.

One of the items they packed with them for their journey was artwork and a manuscript detailing the adventures of a mischievous monkey named Fifi. When Hans and Margarete arrived in New York, a friend connected them with a children's book editor at Houghton Mifflin. Fifi was renamed George, and a four-book contract was signed. The 75th anniversary of the *Curious George* book series took place in 2016 and, to date, more than 75 million copies of the books have been sold worldwide in more than a dozen languages.

Why use this sojourn into literary history to end this chapter? It took courage, hope, determination, and optimism to complete this dangerous trek, and those same qualities are necessary as you try to inspire the aspirational dreams of smart students who don't appear to care very much about anything related to school. By no means am I saying that the underachieving students in your school face the same physical dangers as did the creators of *Curious George*, but the journey these reluctant students must take begins similarly. Someone must help them collect and assemble the spare parts that can ultimately take them on journeys that can lead anywhere.

Like *Curious George* himself, many of your students are impulsive, forgetful, and a constant threat to the status quo. But also like that impish character, if you dig deeply enough, you will find young people who sincerely want to succeed more than fail; to be appreciated by classmates instead of socially sidelined; and to be people whose aspirations carry them into a future filled with more gains than losses.

8

Getting to *A*:
Approachable Educators

Natalie Rimlinger should never have received her PhD from Australian National University (ANU) in 2016. From her recollections, "I was a rebel without a clue at school. By Year 9 it was easier to add up the number of days I was present than the number of absences. By the end of my 10th year, I had done everything possible to piss everybody off. I said 'screw education' and moved away from home" (excerpted from Australian National University, 2016).

Natalie meandered around—literally and figuratively—for years. The daughter of a Vietnam veteran, Natalie eventually began working at the Veterans and Veterans Families Counselling Service and, at age 30, had a conversation with one of their psychologists that changed her life. As Natalie says, "He said to me, 'You know what you're good at?' And I said

'Nothing, I'm hopeless.' And he said, 'You'd make an excellent psychologist because you're human and you've lived through it.'"

Following that conversation, Natalie enrolled in a distance education program, and her first assignment was on the history of emotions. It turned out she wasn't hopeless, as that assignment earned her a grade of 98 percent. With newfound confidence, Natalie transferred to ANU and completed a Bachelor of Science degree in Psychology. When she pursued further options, she looked at doctoral work. "When I first started, I didn't even know what a PhD was, but then I discovered it was the biggest thing you could get. I said, 'I'll have one of those, please.'"

Natalie never did earn her Year 12 Certificate—a high school diploma—and she admits to having nightmares about being on stage at ANU to receive her PhD and being told by a dean that, without that certificate, she was ineligible to receive an advanced degree. Thankfully, that didn't happen.

When Natalie reflects back on her early years of schooling, she does so with both realism and melancholy. "When I look back at school, it all makes sense. I wasn't learning anything. I was bored and demonstrated that boredom by acting out. I was literally the kid voted least likely to do anything worthwhile with their life. Well, you'll have to call me *doctor* now. That seems pretty worthwhile."

Natalie's father was at ANU to see her receive her PhD. He didn't cry, but he showed "his idiot grin," as Natalie calls it. All he said was "Not bad for a kid who didn't get her Year 12 Certificate."

Life preservers aren't just made of cork and polyethylene; they can also be composed of skin and bones—people in our lives who, in ways both grand and small, make us see in ourselves something long hidden by past experiences. Recall the song "Tin Man" by the band *America*? "Oz never did give nothing to the Tin Man that he didn't already have." It might just take an outsider—an educator, psychologist, or personal friend—to point out that truth.

Natalie Rimlinger found this human life preserver in a coworker. Throughout this book, I have offered examples of other lifesavers—individuals who have given hope to someone (maybe many someones) who needed a booster shot of confidence. In this final chapter, I've saved the best for last. Of all of the possible interventions or modifications that could be made in schools to benefit highly able but low-achieving students, the single most important factor is a personal one: the teacher.

In Chapter 6, I mentioned Purkey and Novak's work on invitational education. In a way, this chapter builds on their powerful foundation and adds more texture and depth to things that all educators do to engage students like Natalie—those who are "least likely to do anything worthwhile with their life." Let's begin this reflective journey.

Approachable Educator Strategy 1: Understand the Importance of Psychological Small Change

You have one at home, I'd bet. A jar or box where you toss in all of the loose change you've accumulated over the course of a day. A quarter here, a dime there—fairly meaningless and of little value . . . until you add it up at the end of the year. That petty pocket change will likely have grown into a substantial sum, perhaps enough to splurge on a fancy dinner or new outfit or buy you a plane ticket to someplace fun. What began as just a bunch of tossaway coins grew into something more than just small change; it became guilt-free mad money you could spend or share at will.

Psychological small change can have the same power and impact. It is the unexpected greeting you give in the hall to a student who looks forlorn. It is the close-in parking space you give to another driver on a rainy day. It is the dollar you slip to a hungry 8th grader who forgot her lunch money and has nothing to eat. It is the hug you get from a colleague after you learn about the death of a long-ago, memorable student.

For kids who seldom get recognized for anything worthwhile, this psychological small change can be a value-added asset, paying long-term benefits that might not be immediately recognizable. The trouble is, students like Natalie Rimlinger may be reluctant to accept these acknowledgments or accolades. After all, from their point of view, they have been burned before by educators who made promises they didn't keep, so being willing to trust an adult who says, "I care" or "I'm here for you" might be eyed with more than a small dose of suspicion.

> Throughout my 9+ years of school, I've found that teachers who are patient, receptive, and thoughtful make the best educators. Teachers who are more relaxed and have positive attitudes toward their students take off a lot of pressure, which, in my opinion, is critical to a healthy learning environment.

It's not difficult to understand this initial reluctance; students who may not think very highly of themselves (despite outward bravado) are at a greater risk of feeling betrayed by letting an educator into their private worlds. The key to success with students such as these is perseverance on your part. When you give an invitation to a student that is not accepted (e.g., the kid ignores you or walks away), don't follow the student down the hall to state how rude this behavior was. Chalk it up to initial reluctance on their part and then try again tomorrow . . . and the day after that. It may take numerous attempts before the student is even willing to hear you, so if the verbal strategy doesn't work, try writing a note and handing it to the student privately.

Here's my own personal example. I was a first-year teacher working with students who had many learning challenges. I'd been warned ahead of time by veteran teachers at my school that one of my 6th graders, David, would give me reasons to reconsider my career choice. For the most part, they were right. David had a fine knack for getting under my skin and even more so with the short-fused kids with whom he shared a classroom. There was an abundance of swearing, name calling, and general belligerence (on David's part, not mine!), and I tried my best either to ignore it or to try some of the behavior modification techniques my university professors promised would work.

Unfortunately, they *didn't* work.

One Friday afternoon, after yet another tumultuous week, I called David to my desk while my other students were engaged in some free-time games. I had written a note to David's parents and wanted to share it with him. It read something like this:

I want you to know that I am seeing great progress in David's reading abilities. When I first met David, he seemed reluctant to read at all, but now, whenever I share magazines about nature or outer space, he'll read them from cover to cover. I'm really enjoying having the opportunity to work with your son.

I read the note to David out loud, figuring he might not deliver it to his parents if he didn't know its content. He didn't respond positively or negatively; he just shoved the note in his pocket and promised to give it to his mom and dad.

Then Monday happened.

David came into our classroom earlier than he needed to be there. He didn't say anything. He just sat down at his usual desk.

"Good weekend?" I asked. He nodded yes and then said, "I want to show you something."

At that point, David approached my desk with a photograph of him holding a small, framed object. It was the note I had written to his parents on Friday. David explained that when he gave the note to his parents over dinner, their first thought was 'here we go again . . . another note telling us what David did wrong.' When they read the note's optimistic tone, they made a decision; after dinner, they were going to buy a frame and hang the note in their dining room. It was the first positive note David had ever received from a teacher.

Indeed, psychological small change at work.

David's behavior didn't improve overnight. He still had outbursts and an extensive vocabulary of curse words he used liberally, but since he and I had connected positively early in the year, talking with him about these inappropriate behaviors became easier—for both of us. From his point of view (and mine), we were on the same page. We were looking for ways in which David could succeed.

Carol Ann Tomlinson (2001) knows that these small interactions can yield powerful and positive results. She's highlighted six strategies that, when packaged together, turn psychological small change into a treasure trove:

1. **Study your students.** Take a minute every day to remember that those tennis shoes are attached to lives, each one filled with stories, dreams, and warts.

2. **Develop a taste for kids you find least attractive.** When students see teachers accepting of kids who are prickly or even outcasts, the model and the message are huge.

3. **Give each student opportunities to be the center of your universe.** Small things, like greeting students at the door or recognizing a new haircut, show them that you care about them as people, not just as students.

4. **Watch your students and reflect aloud.** See what happens when you say, "As I've watched you recently, you've taught me something I hadn't understood before." No doubt, your students will sit up a little straighter and want to know more.

5. **Set goals that are a little scary for your students.** There is little more ennobling than realizing than a person you respect believes you are better or more capable than you yourself believe.

6. **Scaffold success.** Ask your students, "What is the next step you'll be taking in your work, and what do you need me to do

in class to make sure you have the knowledge and skills to do an outstanding job?"

Psychological small change reaps benefits far beyond the classroom, including in faculty meetings, where sharing personal triumphs is encouraged; at recess, when you thank a popular student who has asked a social outlier to join the kickball team; and in the cafeteria, where the caretakers of that tumultuous place—the lunch aides—are given a shout out for their hard work that often goes unrecognized.

Without a doubt, psychological small change is the gift that keeps on giving, reaping benefits that make school a little more welcoming and a little less scary for those who need a boost to feel important and valued.

Approachable Educator Strategy 2: Make a Conscious Effort to Diminish the Role of Labels and Limits

If you consider the various educational terms many of our students wear, you come up with an alphabet soup of labels: OCD, ADHD, ODD, LD, G/T. The list goes on and on. Add to these labels some others that students give one another (e.g., jock, athlete, stoner, nerd) and you have a mélange of characteristics that align with various educational and social expectations that aren't always accurate. For instance, some "stoners" are gifted and some students with ADHD can be incredible athletes. Still, reliant as we seem to be on labeling students with various conditions or proclivities, we often put stock in a label's importance without even knowing very much about the student who was assigned that tag.

Educators are also apt to place limits on what students know or are able to do based on either their age or grade-level placement. For example, one of the biggest controversies in the gifted education field involves acceleration, whether it's grade skipping, early entrance to kindergarten, or early graduation from high school. All manner of assumptions are made about the "wrongness" of acceleration, especially as to how it will stunt the social and emotional growth of those unfortunate enough to be placed above where they are "supposed to be" by age. There is virtually no evidence (other than some anecdotal cases) of acceleration as a practice being inherently harmful (Colangelo, Assouline, & Gross, 2004), yet many educators assume that it is.

Some labels can be helpful; indeed, some are required to gain access to educational services. Having a general idea of what students in a certain grade or subject should know and be able to do can also be a helpful benchmark for students whose intellectual development mirrors their age. However, the many outliers to these expectations are reason enough to reexamine our own potential prejudices brought about by labels and limits.

Let's examine two teachers who didn't let limits or labels stop them. In Alec Greven's 3rd grade class in Castle Rock, Colorado, his teacher's assignment seemed pretty direct: choose a topic of interest, research it, and compose your thoughts in a spiral-bound notebook. Alec decided to learn more about boy-girl relationships, because there seemed to be some tension between the sexes at recess. His "book" was seven pages of ideas about not showing off or clowning around in class. He even had some advice for the heartbroken: "Sometimes, you get a girl to like you and then she ditches you. Life is hard, move on."

> You have those excruciatingly painful-to-listen-to teachers that make you wish you had not been born, but then you have the opposite end of the spectrum: those who make you look forward to coming to school. Either type teaches you something unintentionally. The former teaches patience and endurance, while the latter helps you to become yourself.

Alec's teacher, Anna Dupree, thought his book was both hilarious and helpful. It was certainly more than she ever expected from a 9-year-old. She shared Alec's book with the principal and made a copy for the school librarian, who made additional copies to sell at the school's book fair (where all 75 copies were sold)! The school secretary bought one of those copies and sent it to Denver's local news station where a news anchor decided to do a story on Alec's book for a Valentine's Day feature. A colleague sent a tape of Alec's story to the *Ellen* show and, within a week, Alec appeared with DeGeneres on TV.

At the time, Ellen promised to line him up with a New York publisher. She did, and HarperCollins decided to expand on and publish Alec's book, which became a *New York Times* best-seller titled *How to Talk to Girls* (Greven, 2008). This was followed by several additional books, including *How to Talk to Dads* and *How to Talk to Moms*. To add to this story, Alec decided to give a substantial portion of his royalties to an organization called Stand Up to Cancer, since both of his grandmothers were afflicted with this disease.

This tsunami of amazing small events that changed a child's life forever began with a single teacher looking beyond the limits of what a 3rd grader could do. Ms. Dupree might never have thought that this small project would culminate in the smashing success that it became, but by looking beyond the classroom and allowing the limits to be set by someone other than herself—in this case, a 9-year-old boy, a school secretary, Ellen DeGeneres, and HarperCollins—she gave Alec a gift he will never forget: the gift of the possible.

In 2016, Alec was selected as the Rotary Club Student of the Month at Castle View High School, and his principal, Rex Carr, called him a humble and caring person. With a 4.24 GPA and eight AP courses under his belt, Alec is looking at a career in law.

Perhaps Alec's high school success would have occurred anyway—there's no way of knowing the impact of today's words or actions on tomorrow's achievements—but the decision by his 3rd grade teacher to unharness the limitations that others may have imposed due to his age is proof enough that as an educator, letting go is sometimes preferable to holding on.

In a similar vein is first-year teacher Janice Anderson Connolly's story, which she related in the remarkable book *The First Year of Teaching: Real World Stories from America's Teachers* (Kane, 1991). Not only is her story about her first year of teaching, it's about her first *day* as a teacher.

All was going well until 7th period when Janice heard a piece of furniture crash against the wall. Upon entering her high school class, she found two boys fighting on the floor. Her call to stop the fighting sounded tinny and weak, but the fisticuffs stopped as a veteran teacher from across the hall came in and yelled at the entire class (who were all labeled as special education students). At the end of class, Janice stopped Mark, one of the boys who had been fighting, who informed her to simply give up: "Lady, don't waste your time. We're the retards," Mark said.

At this point, what would you do, as either a new teacher or an administrator giving advice to a neophyte educator? Should Janice concentrate on her other classes, all of which had gone well, and simply figure out ways to make it through each day's final period? That's what some teachers thought and told Janice to do exactly that. She didn't buy it.

On the second day, she walked into the last period and wrote one word on the board: *ECINAJ*. She asked her students to read it out loud; it was her name. They were confused until she mentioned that, as a student herself, she had been labeled as dyslexic and couldn't even write her own first name correctly.

"So, how'd you become a teacher?" they asked.

Janice responded that she refused to be held back by labels imposed on her by others and that if they, her students, wanted to accept the labels they had been given, then they should withdraw from her class now. As an alternative, she offered this as an incentive to stay.

"You *will* graduate, and I hope some of you will go to college. That's not a joke or a threat but a promise. I don't *ever* want to hear the word *retard* in this room again. Do you understand?"

Apparently, they did, for at the end of the school year, when Janice mentioned that she was getting married and moving out of state, each of her classes pitched in to buy her flowers. Seventh period, though, had students with little excess cash; however, since Mark worked weekends for a florist, he was able to help in a rather unique way.

On the last day of classes, the principal met Janice at the school's entrance and informed her that there was a problem in her room. When she arrived, her last period students awaited her: "Miss Anderson, Period 2 got you roses and Period 3 got you a corsage, but we love you more." As she entered the classroom, she spied funeral sprays in each corner, bouquets on the filing cabinets, and a funeral blanket draped across her desk. She cried; so did they. Two years later, all of those students graduated, and six earned college scholarships.

Years after that, Janice once again crossed paths with Mark. Married to his college sweetheart and a successful businessman, Mark now had a son of his own who ended up in Janice's sophomore Honors English class. By refusing to place limits so often imposed by labels, Janice Connolly did what every teacher who has ever taught hopes to do: make students aware of the possibilities that reside inside of them.

These two stories prove once again that the main purpose of teaching lies not with the curriculum but within the individual relationships that develop when barriers are broken and limits are ignored. With students who underachieve, these aspects of the educational endeavor are vital cogs in the engine of learning that can either stall or speed up, depending on the interactions between teachers and their students.

Scholar and author Alfie Kohn (2005) knows this well and presents the following scenario:

Imagine that your students are invited to respond to a questionnaire several years after leaving your school. They are asked to indicate whether they agree or disagree with this statement: "Even when I wasn't proud of how I acted, even when I didn't do the homework, even when I got low test scores or didn't seem interested in what was being taught, I knew that *(insert your name here)* still cared about me."

How would you like your students to answer this question? How do you think they will answer it? (p. 24)

Of all of the pieces of assessment data we might collect, is there any one piece more important than the answer to Kohn's questions?

Approachable Educator Strategy 3: Find the Time to Listen to Students

In my almost 40-year career as an educator, I've done my share of public speaking at conferences. Often, instead of keeping the podium and microphone to myself, I share it with a panel of middle or high school students, asking them to share their impressions of school, teachers, their current lives, and their future goals. What astonishes me most is not what the students have to say but how the audience (of teachers, counselors, and administrators) responds. Collectively, they're fully engaged. They take notes and ask for elaboration on students' comments. It's almost as if these participants, most of whom work with or for students daily, have forgotten how beneficial it is to hear from the consumers of our instructional efforts.

This particular approachable educator strategy is straightforward: gather a group of students together and ask them to provide a status report on what they are (or are not) learning in school. When you include underachievers or selective consumers in the mix, you're likely to hear some things that sting, along with some things that make you proud to be an educator. In either case, you will have created a dialogue that both reinforces your hunches on what works with kids and provides suggestions on what could be done better.

One effort to corral such responses arrived decades ago in a book titled *On Being Gifted* (American Association for Gifted Children, 1978), the first book about being gifted or talented that was written by authors who were themselves gifted or talented. The book was the result of a weekend retreat at which 20 gifted high school students wrote down their thoughts on various topics related to giftedness. As written in the preface, the book "is the voice of a friend who doesn't have all the answers but who has walked this path a few steps ahead of you" (p. vi). The student comments are stunningly precise and introspective, and they are as relevant today as when they were written more than a generation ago.

- Being gifted, I have a strong sense of future, because people are always telling me how well I will do when I grow up. . . . My feelings fluctuate from a sense of responsibility for everything to a kind of 'leave me alone—quit pushing.' (p. 7)
- [With my grades] I'd come so close with so little effort. I knew my English and history classes were not challenging. I knew all my teachers were not challenging me. I knew their skies were not my skies. (p. 12)
- In a high school of 1,800 students, I really did not expect to receive very much individual attention; in fact, my whole attitude was pretty bad. My counselor visited with me about my ability and about the importance of really working in high school. His interest in me persisted until I really began to believe that I could go to him with any problem or question. (pp. 61–62)

Having read these student comments decades ago, as I was completing my doctorate in educational psychology, I began to see the benefits of asking my middle and high school aged students what I (and other teachers) do well and how we can improve our interactions with them. Several books that I subsequently wrote or coauthored included comments from thousands of students we either knew personally or connected with through our interactive website at www.giftedkidspeak.com (Delisle, 1991; Schultz & Delisle, 2007, 2013).

This idea of collecting advice from students about the teaching/learning process is one I continue to explore. Some anonymous quotes from 9th graders with whom I have recently worked include such sage advice and observations as the following, in response to my question, "How can teachers do the best job possible to help you navigate the world of learning and schooling?"

- "At age 12, I lost my grandmother to cancer. When I came back to school, I was still sad about it and my English grade dropped to a *C*. My English teacher had me stay after class one day and talked with me. She supported me and truly cared about me. I brought my grade back to an *A* shortly thereafter, as she showed me that she truly cared about me as a person."
- "The pressure to achieve has made school unenjoyable. Sometimes, too much is asked of students at the same time by multiple teachers. I've found that teachers who can balance learning and enjoyment have been most helpful in my academic successes."
- "Teachers should understand that different people learn in different ways. They can't just say something once or give a single example and expect every student to immediately remember or understand."
- "When teachers have a sense of humor, it really helps me to stay focused and learn better. Making little jokes and making me laugh keeps me happy and willing to learn."
- "Teachers need to care about their lessons and be passionate about them, not just throw a stack of papers in my face and say, "Just do this." If the teacher doesn't care, then why should I?"

- "I never really thought teachers cared until 7th grade. I was never good at math, and a big test was coming up. I went to my teacher's classroom for tutoring every day. After the test results came out, she called me to her room and told me I had received a grade of 100 percent. I guess what I'm trying to say is that a connection is needed between students and teachers. In my case, even with hundreds of other students, my math teacher gave me this gift of time."

Approachable teachers allow you to build a relationship where the primary goal is success. They show that they actually care about their students and are not there just to be there.

One of the most efficient venues for raising issues that connect us with our students is a "lunch bunch" format where students are invited to participate in open-ended discussions such as these, generally during their lunch break. Participation is entirely voluntary and students may choose to attend as many or as few sessions as they wish. (Initially, I suggest holding these sessions twice monthly.) An adult can moderate the first few discussions, transferring the leadership role in subsequent sessions to a willing student who wishes to raise particular issues. It's appropriate to establish some ground rules that respect the individuality that will likely emerge through student comments, and it's also appropriate to mention what things will not be tolerated, such as foul language, disrespect, name calling, or calling out anyone—student or teacher—by name. EdChange (2015), an organization that focuses on positive change in school and beyond, has developed a set of ground rules for group discussions that are specific and logical, including

- Only one person speaks at a time.
- Speak from your own experience, using *I* instead of *they* or *we*.

- Don't "hijack" someone else's story by making it a segue into your own example. Instead, stick with the other person's example and ask for more details.
- Watch your body language, for it can be as disrespectful as words.

A guiding precept that can be shared at the onset of each lunch bunch discussion is a quote from author Matthew Kelly (2007): "The more each person can remove his or her ego from the discussion and focus on the subject matter, the more fruitful the conversation will be for all involved" (p. 157).

As a closing thought to this strategy, remember this: one need not be a trained counselor to conduct lunch bunch discussions. Rather, an individual who truly wants to know what students think about their lives in and outside of school is the most essential prerequisite for success.

Approachable Educator Strategy 4: Understand the Unexpected Consequences of Praise

High-achieving gifted students have this happen all the time. They get praised for their straight-*A* report cards, their oversized brains, and their amazingly strong academic prowess. They get so much praise, in fact, that many smart students become addicted to the glowing words of others to such a degree that they forego activities and school options where praise is not offered as a reward. In essence, they become "praise junkies." A byproduct of this addiction is that high-achieving students tie their self-concept to this awarding of praise. The result is students who believe they are only worthwhile when they are performing on all eight academic cylinders.

What follows should not be surprising: smart students may eschew anything that makes them appear less than brilliant. With underachievers, the need to be perfect is so strong that the desire to work on anything that might not be deemed excellent by others is moribund. I know I've traveled down this path before in this book, but my reiteration here is intentional, as I wish to add another thread to the complex tapestry of reasons why some smart students choose to do poorly on purpose. Specifically, it's time to reappraise praise.

In a classic article from the *Harvard Business Review*, Richard Farson (1963) examined the negative effects of praise on recipients, suggesting that among its problems are these:

- Praise is often seen as an evaluation, implying that its recipient may be found deficient in the future if such a high level of performance is not maintained.
- Praise may be interpreted as a call to change or improve beyond one's current level of functioning (e.g., "Geez . . . good job! Almost perfect, in fact!"), causing praise to be seen more as an implied threat than as a genuine reward.
- Praise assumes that the person giving the accolades is more accomplished than its recipient, which may be an unconscious way to show the superiority of the praiser.
- Praise is often used artificially to "sandwich" bad news, causing the recipient to wonder if the praise is even legitimate or just a sneaky, face-saving way for the praiser to get you to improve in the future.
- Praise may restrict creativity if the only thing responded to positively is the "correctness" of the praiseworthy effort, rather than its innovative elements.

Another aspect of praise that makes it more hollow than solid is that most of it is so general in nature that the person getting praised hasn't a clue as to what specifically was praiseworthy. Comments such as "Nice job" or "You did excellent work" are so vague as to be purposeless.

On the other hand, if a positive statement of praise is phrased differently, it might have a stronger impact beyond a mere pat on the back. Adding some specificity with statements such as "These are the reasons I appreciate your work so much . . ." or "I think it was extraordinarily effective to have the voice of your story's narrator appear only twice" invites the recipient to continue a dialogue that might not otherwise take place.

Another technique that is guaranteed to continue the dialogue—rather than stunt it—is to ask the student to reflect on the quality of his or her own work. Saying something like, "I have a few comments on specific parts of your assignment that I found enlightening, but I'm curious to hear what you think are the best aspects of this work" is likely to get the student to examine the completed project more closely. Initially, the response you get might be "I don't know . . . I just did what you told me," but if you follow up with a gentle nudge to get the student to look more closely at a project's most impressive parts, the conversation will eventually flow. For underachievers who may not be the most expressive among your students, this casual and honest dialogue about something they did well may be the key to convincing them that their efforts are valued.

One final thing about praise: most of us are somewhat dismissive when we receive it ourselves. More often than not, when someone tells us that they like something we did, we respond with statements such as "It really isn't that great" or "If I had more time to work on it, it could've been better." Here's a hint. Instead of dismissing another's words of praise, practice saying thank you. Praise, if given genuinely and specifically, can be a boost to even the biggest of egos. A simple thank you allows both the praiser and the praisee to have their efforts acknowledged.

Approachable Educator Strategy 5: Create Your Own Potpourri of Strategies

A potpourri can be many things—a sweetly scented bundle of lavender, a medley of musical compositions, or a patchwork of related ideas. It is this latter definition that will guide the suggestions that follow.

Let's start with another story. Dick Jordan was a high school teacher in the Denver, Colorado, public school system for more than 30 years. He ended each year the same way he ended his first: by telling his students that he wanted them to show up at the Denver Public Library's main branch on January 1, 2000. He instructed them each to bring him a dollar that day. The reason for his request? If every student he taught throughout his career gave Dick a dollar, he'd have enough money to bring his wife on a vacation to Tahiti.

When that auspicious new millennial date arrived, Dick and his wife showed up at the appointed place at the appointed time . . . and so did more than 100 of Dick's former students who had collected more than $750. Unfortunately, even this generous outpouring wasn't enough to get Dick and his wife to Tahiti, so they donated the money to the Catholic Workers Soup Kitchen. Shortly thereafter, the Tahiti Tourist Board, Air France, and Delta Airlines heard about Dick's story, and they sent Dick and his wife on an all-expenses-paid vacation of a lifetime.

There is as much beauty in this story as there is sand in Tahiti. Of course, the corporate sponsors need to be applauded for their thoughtfulness and generosity. Likewise, the former students who showed up to celebrate the career of a long-ago teacher are to be recognized. Most of all, though, it is Dick Jordan who is at the centerpiece of this tale. To be bold enough to make the same request from each of his students for more than 30 years, and to be brave enough to arrive at the library not knowing if anyone else would even show up, is evidence enough that this man did more than simply teach his subject. He taught people. He did this so effectively, in fact, that more than 100 of them could not *not* show up on the day that an unforgettable teacher asked them to.

I don't know Dick Jordan personally, but I've been lucky enough to have had a couple of teachers as memorable as he was to his own students. They all brought a potpourri of strategies to their instruction that prompted me to want to learn more, go beyond the basics, and succeed as much for them as for myself. For students who underachieve or do poorly on purpose, such individuals are as rare as they are precious, so when they find them, they cling to them as strongly as Velcro to wool.

Here are some additional strategies that might just convince reluctant learners that someone in school actually cares about who they are and what they think.

Tabula Rasa. This is a Latin term that translates to "blank slate." Philosophical empiricists use this term to describe the human mind before ideas have been imprinted on it by outside forces. In this activity, students who participate will not be blank slates at all; instead, they will be a collective of opinions, judgments, and ideas based on what has already occurred in their lives. Still, if students complete this activity by jotting down the very first thoughts that come to mind after reading the prompt, their minds will be as blank (and honest) as they can possibly be. Here are some suggested prompts to set your students' minds ablaze:

- If I could change one thing about my life . . .
- When I consider my future . . .
- My social life . . .
- I do best in school when . . .
- I do worst in school when . . .
- When I do well in school . . .
- When I do poorly in school . . .
- If I could convince my teachers of one thing . . .
- Most of my friends expect me to . . .
- When I consider my parents . . .
- The thing I care about the most . . .
- If I could change high school . . .
- My favorite teachers are the ones who . . .
- The most interesting aspect of my life is . . .
- A song title that describes me well is . . .

In conducting this activity numerous times with hundreds of students, the variety of responses I receive is always intriguing.

Some students take the activity quite seriously, whereas others add so much whimsy that their responses sound like a comedy routine. Here are some examples:

My social life . . .

- is complicated and atypical.
- is busy, saucy, and fun.
- is none of your business.

If I could change one thing about my life . . .

- I wouldn't be sad anymore.
- I'd want my parents to have the lives they'd dreamed of earlier.
- I would spend less time in school.
- I would be taller.

When I do well in school . . .

- nobody cares—that's what others expect.
- I feel I've avoided failure one more time.
- I keep it to myself.

When I don't do well in school . . .

- nobody cares—that's what others expect.
- I question if I'm as smart as people say I am.
- I tell myself no one will ever grade me again after I graduate.

An activity like this is a great ice-breaker for one of the "lunch bunch" discussion sessions mentioned earlier. Students can be invited to share responses in a round-robin fashion (with the option of passing, if they choose) and can also be invited to compose their own sentence stems they want their classmates to consider. Another twist on this activity is to do it twice in the same year—at the beginning of the school year and again near the end. In past years, I've collected students' initial responses and filed them away. Then, with only weeks to go in the school year, I give students the same questions before distributing their original responses. We then discuss the differences and similarities between the two sets. Are some more optimistic or pessimistic? Are some new responses nearly identical to ones written earlier in the year? What changes in thinking are most obvious?

If you want honest discussion about topics relevant to your students' lives, the Tabula Rasa activity is one that will open up conversations that might not occur otherwise.

A Nod to Ernest Hemingway. It all began with a bet. Ernest Hemingway was speaking with a friend about the benefits of writing in his style: clean, terse, direct. His friend challenged Hemingway to a $10 wager: write a complete story in exactly six words. Not chapters. Not paragraphs. Not sentences. Just six words.

Hemingway won the bet by composing this story: "For sale. Baby shoes. Never worn."

Years later, this oft-told tale was reimagined by several entrepreneurs in California who decided to launch *SMITH Magazine*. They believed that both everyday and famous people would be willing to share their life stories—but in only and exactly six words. Their idea paid off, and they published several anthologies of six-word stories that became best sellers (e.g., Fershieleiser & Smith, 2008). Since then, they've also developed an app and have been featured in media as diverse as *Los Angeles Times*, *The New York Times*, *Entertainment Weekly*, and National Public Radio. The stories lead to reflection and discussion, and this activity is one you might want to include as you engage students in a bit of self-reflection as they review the ups and downs of their own lives.

In conducting this activity, I begin by telling students of its Hemingway genesis and its subsequent adoption by *SMITH Magazine*. Then I offer several categories in which students can compose their own six-word life stories:

- My life as a student
- My life as an athlete
- My life as an artist
- My life in general

- My greatest triumph
- My biggest defeat
- My advice to others
- My advice to myself

Responses from middle and high school students with whom I've worked include the following:

- Basics for survival: eat, sleep, swim.
- Dreams held tightly. Even when broken.
- I wonder what this button does?
- Music reaches people. I make music.
- Sunny with a chance of rain.
- Does hope always work like this?
- Raised my sister before raising myself.
- Worked and chiseled but still imperfect.
- Dark, dramatic, disturbing, poetic: my life.

Initially, I didn't think—and neither did my students—that this six-word activity would have any meaningful significance, yet it does. Perhaps, as Hemingway discovered, there is a particular form of magic in brevity. It leads to personal interpretation (Why exactly *were* those baby shoes never worn?), introspective analysis, and a desire to hear more about what the story entails beyond the six written words. Even your most reluctant writers are unlikely to cringe at the idea of composing only six words. It may be the easiest assignment to complete yet still one of the most profoundly affecting writing exercises you'll ever do.

Last Words. A former 7th grader I came to know, Kenny, was sitting in his special ed class, bored as usual, when his teacher asked me to come in and talk with him. She'd not known Kenny very long, yet she recognized there was something different about him. His writing was almost indecipherable due to his grammar, syntax, and spelling errors, but the ideas he raised in class seemed very advanced. It took only a few minutes talking with Kenny for me to realize that his intellect was stronger than his academic efforts indicated, and his knowledge of history and current events rivaled that of most adults. Long story short: Kenny had dyslexia and, even with that disability, managed to score 129 on a group-administered IQ test. Kenny was the poster child for students we have come to call "twice exceptional"—gifted individuals with an identified learning disability. Kenny and I continued to work together for almost two years.

Near the end of 8th grade, Kenny presented me with a gift: the current issue of *Skateboarding* magazine. My puzzled look amused Kenny, who assumed (correctly) that I'd never read this magazine before. "Turn to the last page," he instructed. When I did, I found an article titled "Last Words," which was an interview, of sorts, with a famous skateboarder.

"When I read this," Kenny informed me, "I thought of a lot of the activities you've done with us. This one seemed to fit in."

It did, and it has become one of my favorite activities to use with students who, like Kenny, have much to share about their lives. Although some of the last word categories in the magazine were devoted to skateboarding twists, tricks, and injuries, most are more general in nature. For example, what or when was . . .

- The last book you started but did not finish.
- The last time you lost something.
- The last time you felt out of place.
- The last time you felt cheated.
- The last time you felt truly happy.
- The last photo you took.
- The last serious miscalculation you made.
- The last time you felt loved.
- The last time you felt envious of someone.
- The last time you wanted to give up.
- The last person who inspired you.
- The last time you cried.
- The last time you laughed.
- The last time you were embarrassed.

- The last award you received.
- The last promise you made.
- The last time you were disappointed.
- The last present you bought for someone.
- The last present someone bought for you.

Rather than have students write their responses to these prompts, I put them in pairs or small groups and have them interview one another. Of course, an answer alone is insufficient, as the backstory is where the truly interesting aspects emerge. Therefore, if the last book you stopped reading was *Heart of Darkness*, why didn't you read further? If the last time you wanted to give up was when you had three tests and a term paper due on the same day, then you are likely to hear groans of agreement.

This activity is best done with the teacher being the "interviewee guinea pig" and initially answering prompts given to them by students. Teachers, like students, have the option of passing and not answering particular questions, but the elaborative comments you make are where the openness emerges and honest communication blossoms. Any instance where we can share our common humanity with students is another step toward building a relationship that will have them seeking you out, perhaps years later, at the Denver Public Library or elsewhere, with a dollar in hand to add to your Tahiti vacation fund.

And that's the last word on this topic.

Summary

Doctor Who is one of the longest-running British television shows and has achieved cult status. An extraterrestrial from the planet Gallifrey, The Doctor has a mission to explore the universe and find ways to save civilizations and help people in need. In his (and now her) extensive travels, The Doctor has come to realize that "900 years of time and space and I've never met anyone who isn't important."

The Doctor is on to something. Even the most reluctant learners in schools need to believe that *someone* within that institution believes they are important. Some students get noticed for their good behaviors and high grades, whereas others get singled out for poor performance and a lousy attitude. But at least both types of students get *some* attention, be it positive or negative. It is my belief that the students who have it the worst in school are the ones who fit into neither of these categories. They are ciphers who get no attention at all, including those who underachieve for reasons as varied as the students themselves.

A single educator or member of the larger school community can engage these children by simply noticing their presence and acknowledging their importance. Someone less alien than The Doctor, writer John Steinbeck, understands the life-changing role of such an educator, as he was privileged enough to have a few of them in his life. Steinbeck (n.d.) wrote,

School is not so easy and it is not for the most part very fun, but then, if you are very lucky, you may find a teacher. Three real teachers in a lifetime is the very best of luck. I have come to believe that a great teacher is a great artist and that there are as few as there are any other great artists. Teaching might even be the greatest of the arts since the medium is the human mind and spirit.

My three had these things in common. They all loved what they were doing. They did not tell—they catalyzed a burning desire to know. Under their influence, the horizons sprung wide and fear went away and the unknown became knowable. But most important of all, the truth, that dangerous stuff, became beautiful and very precious. (paras. 1–2)

Approachable educators bring more to their classrooms than the content they are assigned to teach. *Approachable educators*

offer students insights into their lives by not being afraid to open up parts of their own. *Approachable educators* connect with their students using a genuineness that is grounded in honesty and respect. *Approachable educators* look beyond the messiness, low grades, belligerent comebacks, and neglected assignments and offer this irresistible invitation offered by Carol Ann Tomlinson (2001): "Come see this magic world I love. I care for you so much that I must share it with you" (p. 44).

For many teachers, connecting with students is the most pleasant part of their jobs, reminding them why they chose education as a profession in the first place. But when students make our jobs as educators harder, as underachievers often do, we may question the value of the efforts we put forth that they seem to either ignore or find of little value. When this happens, approachable educators need to continue to remember that the fruits of their labor are not always visible in the short term. Weeks, months, or years later, the extra effort you took to listen, assist, or simply give another chance that may not even have been deserved may pay off in ways you will never see. As one now high-performing student of mine related recently, "Mrs. P. had an absolutely positive attitude about the information she presented, which made me want to be as happy to learn it as she was to share it. Truly, she gave me a passion to learn and taught me to be curious. This passion continues to intensify. Thank you, Mrs. P."

Thank you, indeed.

Epilogue:
A Story with Chapters
Yet to Be Written

There is a crack in everything.
That's how the light gets in.
—Leonard Cohen, "Anthem"

When I began my career as a special education teacher four decades ago, it was in a northern New Hampshire school where recess was canceled anytime a moose showed up on the playground. I had no knowledge that giftedness could coexist with disabilities. Indeed, I had no knowledge about giftedness *at all*. Then I met Matt, the "maple sugar kid" I introduced in this book's preface, who had both high academic abilities and a loathing for a school that didn't care he had them. He was labeled on his IEP as behaviorally disordered, and I took that label seriously. *Too* seriously. I was a neophyte educator who figured that those who came before me and had applied the label knew better than I did about how to reach seemingly unreachable kids like Matt—behavioral objectives, charts documenting Matt's noncompliance with school rules, and punishments for any of his behaviors that disrupted the smooth flow of learning in my classroom. As I mentioned, my first few months of work with Matt were disastrous—for both of us.

Only when I began to see education from Matt's side of the desk did he and I begin to connect. He was capable in many areas I either knew nothing about or seemed (to him) to care little about. But when Matt came to school after he had interrupted a pair of amorous skunks and gotten sprayed, I could no longer ignore him. From that day forward, I came to recognize that Matt had more to offer than what I had given to him through my programmed curriculum. Because I let go of what I thought was best for his education and adopted some of Matt's ideas about what an appropriate curriculum could look like, we reached milestone after milestone. And, along the way, we grew to respect what each of us could learn from the other.

This journey we took together was painful at times but, like most arduous treks that end someplace memorable, the slogs and pitfalls seemed less important once success was achieved. Good things are seldom attained without some degree of struggle, and with Matt and countless other kids like him, getting beyond the inevitable hurdles takes patience, trust, creativity, and care.

Author and educator Neil Postman (1982) wrote that "children are the living messages we send to a time we will not see" (p. xi). This is a gentle yet powerful reminder that the legacy of our efforts on behalf of children will continue to ripple long after our days with them have passed. It should also give us pause to consider the effect of our actions—and inactions—on our students' lives.

Kids like Sierra and Marty—underachievers and selective consumers—need the reassurance that they are capable, valuable, and worth listening to despite their low academic performance. In a word, they want *dignity*. Don't we all?

Getting to *A* is less a function of getting good grades as much as it is giving our most reluctant learners something else: autonomy, access, advocacy, alternatives, aspirations, and most important, approachable educators such as you.

However you come to see things from your students' points of view, whether it's thanks to a skunk or something far less odorous and extreme, take the time to let your underachieving students know that light gets in through even the smallest of cracks.

References

American Association for Gifted Children. (1978). *On being gifted.* New York: Walker and Company.

Asbury, C. (1974). Selected factors influencing over and under-achievement in young school-age children. *Review of Educational Research, 44*, 401–428.

Australian National University. (2016). One grad's bumpy ride to a PhD [blog post]. Retrieved from *Australian National University: Science, Environment, Health & Medicine* at http://science.anu.edu.au/study/career-student-stories/one-grads-bumpy-ride-phd.

Berliner, D. C., & Biddle, B. J. (1995). *The manufactured crisis: Myths, fraud and the attack on America's public schools.* Reading, MA: Addison-Wesley.

Bjork, R. A. (n.d.). Research: Applying cognitive psychology to enhance educational practice. Retrieved from https://bjorklab.psych.ucla.edu/research/#toc.

Borden, L. (2005). *The journey that saved Curious George.* Boston: Houghton Mifflin.

Bradburn, K. (2007). How to prevent another Leonardo da Vinci [blog post]. Retrieved from *Wandering Ink* at http://wanderingink.wordpress.com/2007/05/23/how-to-prevent-another-leonardo-da-vinci.

Branch, B. (2012). Khan Academy. *Gifted Education Communicator, 43*(2), 38–40.

Bridgeland, J. M., Dilulio, J. J., & Morison, K. B. (2006). *The silent epidemic: Perspectives of high school dropouts.* Washington, DC: Civic Enterprises.

Chen, M. (2010). *Education nation: Six leading edges of innovation.* San Francisco: Jossey-Bass.

Clark, B. (2013). *Growing up gifted: Developing the potential of children at home and at school.* New York: Pearson.

Colangelo, N., Assouline, S. G., & Gross, M.U.M. (2004). *A nation deceived: How schools hold back America's brightest students (Vol. 1)*. Iowa City: University of Iowa Press.

College Board. (2017). AP capstone update. Retrieved from http://advancesinap.collegeboard.org/ap-capstone.

Cox, J., Daniel, N., & Boston, B. (1985). *Educating able learners: Programs and promising practices*. Austin: University of Texas Press.

Darling-Hammond, L. (2010). Steady work: Finland builds a strong teaching and learning system. *Rethinking Schools, 24*(4), 30–35.

Delisle, J. R. (1991). *Guiding the social and emotional development of gifted youth*. White Plains, NY: Longman.

Douglas, D. (n.d.). Self advocacy [blog post]. Retrieved from *GT Carpe Diem* at www.gtcarpediem.com/self-advocacy-overview.

Douglas, D. (2018). *The power of self-advocacy for gifted learners: Teaching the four essential steps to success*. Minneapolis, MN: Free Spirit Publishing.

EdChange. (2015). Guide for setting ground rules. Retrieved from www.edchange.org/multicultural/activities/groundrules.html.

Emerick, L. J. (1992). Academic underachievement among the gifted: Students' perceptions of factors that reverse the pattern. *Gifted Child Quarterly, 36*(3), 140–146.

Emerson, R. W. (1883). Education. In *The Works of Ralph Waldo Emerson*. Retrieved from http://archive.vcu.edu/english/engweb/transcendentalism/authors/emerson.

Farson, R. E. (1963). Praise . . . reappraised. *Harvard Business Review, 41*(5), 61–66.

Ferrucci, P. (1982). *What we may be*. Los Angeles: J.P. Tarcher.

Fershieleiser, R., & Smith, L. (2008). *Not quite what I was planning: Six word memoirs by writers famous and obscure*. New York: Harper Perennial.

Fine, B. (1967). *Underachievers: How they can be helped*. New York: Dutton.

Galbraith, J., & Delisle, J. (2011). *The gifted teen survival guide: Smart, sharp, and ready for (almost) anything*. Minneapolis, MN: Free Spirit Publishing.

Galbraith, J., & Delisle, J. (2015). *When gifted kids don't have all the answers: How to meet their social and emotional needs*. Minneapolis, MN: Free Spirit Publishing.

Gallagher, J. J. (1975). *Teaching the gifted child.* Boston: Allyn and Bacon.

Gallup. (2015). Student poll results, 2015. Retrieved from www.gallup.com/services/189926/student-poll-2015-results.aspx.

Gelb, M. (2004). *How to think like Leonardo da Vinci.* New York: Bantam.

Goodlad, J. I. (2003). A nation in wait. *Education Week.* Retrieved from www.edweek.org/ew/articles/2003/04/23/32goodlad.h22.html?qs=john+Goodlad.

Greven, A. (2008). *How to talk to girls.* New York: HarperCollins.

Halsted, J. W. (2009). *Some of my best friends are books: Guiding gifted readers from preschool to high school (3rd ed.).* Scottsdale, AZ: Great Potential Press.

Hanh, T. N. (1992). *Peace is every step.* New York: Bantam.

Heacox, D. (2012). *Differentiating instruction in the regular classroom: How to reach and teach all learners.* Minneapolis, MN: Free Spirit Publishing.

Heacox, D., & Cash, R. M. (2014). *Differentiation for gifted learners: Going beyond the basics.* Minneapolis, MN: Free Spirit Publishing.

Hebert, T. (2006). Guided viewing of film with gifted students: Resources for educators and counselors. *Gifted Child Today, 29*(3), 14–27.

Hildreth, G. (1966). *Introduction to the gifted child.* New York: McGraw-Hill.

Hoyt, K., & Hebeler, J. (1974). *Career education for gifted and talented students.* Salt Lake City, UT: Olympus.

Indiana University. (2010). *National survey of student engagement 2010.* Bloomington, IN: Author.

International Baccalaureate. (n.d.). Mission and strategy. Retrieved from www.ibo.org/mission.

Johns Hopkins Center for Talented Youth. (2017). Academic competitions. Retrieved from www.cty.jhu.edu/imagine/resources/competitions.

Jolly, J. (2009). The National Defense Education Act, current STEM initiative, and the gifted. *Gifted Child Today, 32*(3), 50–53.

Jones, C. (1991). *Mistakes that worked: The world's familiar inventions and how they came to be.* New York: Delacorte.

Kane, P. R. (Ed.) (1991). *The first year of teaching: Real world stories from America's teachers.* London, UK: Walker Books.

Kelly, M. (2007). *The seven levels of intimacy: The art of loving and the joy of being loved.* New York: Beacon.

Kohn, A. (2005). Unconditional teaching. *Educational Leadership, 63*(1), 20–24.

Lieberman, M. (2012). Self-knowledge: From philosophy to neuro-science to psychology. In S. Vazire & T. D. Wilson (Eds.), *Handbook of self-knowledge* (pp. 63–76). New York: Guilford.

Livio, M. (2013). *Brilliant blunders: Colossal mistakes by great scientists that changed our understanding of life and the universe.* New York: Simon and Schuster.

MacKinnon, D. (1978). *In search of human effectiveness.* Buffalo, NY: Creative Education Foundation.

Main, H., & Main, C. (2015). *One candle, one meal: A high schooler's business journal.* (n.p.): Total Fusion Press.

Medvec, V. H., Madey, S.F., & Gilovich, T. (1995). When less is more: Counterfactual thinking and satisfaction among Olympic medalists. *Journal of Personality and Social Psychology, 69*(4), 603–610.

Miron, G., & Gulosino, C. (2016). *Virtual schools report 2016.* Boulder, CO: National Education Policy Center.

Mrazek, M. D., Franklin, M. S., Phillips, D. T, Baird, B., & Schooler, J. W. (2013). Mindfulness training improves working memory capacity and GRE performance while reducing mind wandering. *Psychological Science, 20*(10), 1–6.

National Commission on Excellence in Education. (1983). *A nation at risk: The imperative for educational reform.* Washington, DC: U.S. Government Printing Office.

National History Day. (2016). Why NHD works. Retrieved from www.nhd.org/why-NHD/works.

Organisation for Economic Co-operation and Development. (2000). *Student engagement at school: A sense of belonging and participation.* Retrieved from www.oecd.org/edu/school/programmeforinternationalstudentassessmentpisa/33689885.pdf.

Peterson, J. S. (2008). *The essential guide to talking with gifted teens: Ready-to-use discussions about identity, stress, relationships and more.* Minneapolis, MN: Free Spirit Publishing.

Postman, N. (1982). *The disappearance of childhood.* New York: Delacort.

Pringle, M. L. (1970). *Able misfits: A study of educational and behavior difficulties of 103 very intelligent children (IQs 120–200).* London: Longman.

Purkey, W. W., & Novak, J. J. (1984). *Inviting school success (2nd ed.).* Belmont, CA: Wadsworth.

Raph, J. B., Goldberg, M. L., & Passow, A. H. (1966). *Bright underachievers: Studies of scholastic underachievement among intellectually superior high school students.* New York: Teachers College Press.

Raph, J. B., & Tannenbaum, A. J. (1961). *Underachievement: Review of literature.* New York: Teachers College Press.

Renzulli, J. S., & Smith, L. (1978). *The compactor.* Mansfield, CT: Creative Learning Press.

Rimm, S. B. (2008). *Why bright kids get poor grades and what you can do about it: A six-step program for parents and teachers.* Tucson, AZ: Great Potential Press.

Roeper School Board of Trustees. (2013). Educational statement of purpose. Retrieved from http://Roeper.org/general-information/educational-statement-of-purpose.

Rotter, J. B. (1966). Generalized expectations for internal versus external control of reinforcement. *Psychological Monographs: General and Applied, 80*(1), 1–28.

Rotter, J. B. (1990). Internal versus external control of reinforcement: A case history of a variable. *American Psychologist, 45,* 489–493.

Ruff, M. (2016). *The origins of The Roeper School.* Bloomfield Hills, MI: The Roeper School.

Sadler, P. M., Sonnert, G., Tai, R. H., & Klopfenstein, K., Eds. (2010). *AP: A critical examination of the Advanced Placement program.* Cambridge, MA: Harvard University Press.

Sayler, M. F. (2009). Locus of control. In *Encyclopedia of giftedness, creativity, and talent,* Barbara Kerr (Ed.), pp. 540–541. Thousand Oaks, CA: Sage.

Schultz, R. A., & Delisle, J. R. (2007). *More than a test score: Teens talk about being gifted, talented, or otherwise extra-ordinary.* Minneapolis, MN: Free Spirit Publishing.

Schultz, R. A., & Delisle J. R. (2013). *If I'm so smart, why aren't the answers easy?* Waco, TX: Prufrock Press Publishing.

Snyder, T. D., & Dillon, S. A. (2015). *Digest of educational statistics, 2013.* Washington, DC: U.S. Government Printing Office.

Steinbeck, J. (n.d.). On teaching. Retrieved from www.rjgeib.com/thoughts/truth/on-teaching.html.

Strang, R. (1960). *Helping your gifted child.* New York: Dutton.

TED. (n.d.) History of TED. Retrieved from www.ted.com/about/our-organization/history-of-ted.

Tomlinson, C. A. (2001). How to connect with kids. *Gifted Education Communicator, 32*(2), 42–44.

Tomlinson, C. A. (2017). *How to differentiate instruction in academically diverse classrooms, 3rd Edition.* Alexandria, VA: ASCD.

Torrance. (n.d.). Torrance quotes [blog post]. Retrieved from *Torrance Center Oklahoma* at http://torrancecentertulsa.org/6.html.

Tynan-Wood, C. (2016). The reality of virtual schools [blog post]. Retrieved from *Great Schools* at www.greatschools.org/gk/articles/virtual-schools.

U.S. Department of Education. (2008). *A nation accountable: 25 years after* A Nation at Risk. Retrieved from www2.ed.gov/rschstat/research/pubs/accountable/accountable.pdf.

Van Gemert, L. (2017). *Perfectionism: A practical guide for managing 'never good enough.'* Tucson, AZ: Great Potential.

Whitmore, J. R. (1980). *Giftedness, conflict, and underachievement.* Boston: Allyn and Bacon.

Williamson, M. (1992). *A return to love.* New York: HarperCollins.

Index

The letter *f* following a page number denotes a figure.

About the Author

Dr. James (Jim) R. Delisle has taught gifted children and those who work on their behalf for more than 39 years. Jim retired from Kent State University in 2008 after 25 years of service there as a distinguished professor of special education. Throughout his career, Jim has taken time away from college teaching to return to his "classroom roots," volunteering as a 2nd, 4th, 5th, and 8th grade teacher in 1991, 1997, and 2006. Jim has also taught gifted middle school students one day a week between 1998–2008 in the Twinsburg, Ohio, public schools. For the past six years, Jim has worked part time with highly gifted 9th and 10th graders at the Scholars' Academy in Conway, South Carolina.

The author of more than 250 articles and 20 books, Jim's work has been translated into multiple languages and has been featured in both professional journals and popular media, such as *The New York Times*, *People*, and on *Oprah!* A frequent presenter throughout the United States, Jim has also addressed audiences in nations as diverse as the United Kingdom, Greece, China, Oman, Turkey, New Zealand, United Arab Emirates, and Saudi Arabia.

 Free Spirit Publishing is the leading publisher of learning tools that support young people's social-emotional health and educational needs. We provide educators with practical, high-quality resources to support them in helping students think for themselves, overcome challenges, and make a difference in the world.